Tom McNally's Complete Book of
Fishermen's Knots

Tom McNally's Complete Book of

Fishermen's Knots

By Tom McNally

Compiled by Bob McNally

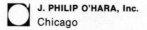

J. PHILIP O'HARA, Inc.
Chicago

J. Philip O'Hara, Inc. 20 East Huron, Chicago 60611.
Published simultaneously in Canada by Van Nostrand Reinhold Ltd.,
Scarborough, Ontario.

LC Number 73–20850
ISBN: 0-87955-420-7 Casebound
ISBN: 0-87955-406-1 Paper
First Printing B

Contents

Tom McNally's Complete Book of

Fishermen's Knots

Introduction

One spring day an Illinois Conservation Officer watched a fisherman at Chicago's Montrose Harbor battle a huge coho salmon he had hooked on a worm. After 15 minutes, the fisherman had the salmon at his feet, laying played out on its side by the Montrose breakwater. The fisherman reached down, grabbed the line just up from the hook, and started to draw the heavy fish toward him. Just then the coho gave a final flop—and wriggled free. The fisherman's knot had pulled loose at the hook!

"That was about the saddest thing I'd ever seen," the warden reported. "I'm sure that coho was 20 or 22 pounds, the biggest fish that guy had ever seen. Tears welled up in his eyes when he watched that salmon roll away."

Another day a fly fisherman cast to the largest bone fish he'd ever seen on the flats at Great Exuma in the Bahamas. The fish inhaled the fly and took off on a typical, lightning-fast bone fish run. Fly line zipped through the guides; then came the backing; then everything went slack. The knot connecting the fly line to the backing line didn't hold—and not only did the saddened fisherman lose a prize bone fish, but he also lost a $16 fly line.

And still another day a wealthy businessman with his own offshore cruiser, captain, and mate was trolling off Brielle, New Jersey for broadbill swordfish. Broadbill are scarce, elusive, difficult to hook, and are tough fighting fish. The businessman was lucky enough to hook a good one, but after a half hour the line went limp. When he reeled in he saw that the wire leader, rigged by the captain and mate, had pulled loose from a swivel. The businessman fired both the captain and mate on the spot!

The three examples of trophy fish lost because of knot failure presented here are typical of zillions of similar incidents that occur to fisherman around the world. Every season, thousands upon thousands of sought-after fish are lost because some fisherman did not tie the right knot—or he tied the right knot wrong!

The sad part of it all is that there is no need for trophy or prize fish, or even for ordinary fish, to be lost because of poor knots. Anyone can learn to tie good, dependable knots.

Al McClane, Executive Editor of *Field and Stream Magazine* and one of our most knowledgeable fishermen, once wrote that a knot is "a means of fastening together the parts of one or more flexible materials such as rope, line, or leader, or of fastening such material to a stanchion, mast, or cleat. Knots include bends, hitches, and splices."

That is as good a definition of a knot as is possible, only it doesn't help the fisherman who wants to learn how to tie one. When Mr. McClane was defining what a knot *is*, he wasn't giving instruction in how to tie them.

For every angler, and most particularly for the serious angler, the ability to tie proper fishing knots is vitally important. It is one of the most important factors to fishing success. When all other things are normal, the fisherman's knots are the weakest part of his equipment. More prize fish are lost because knots pull out, slip, or cut themselves than are lost because of a broken line or faulty tackle. Knot tying may be somewhat unimportant in fishing for panfish, since they do not exert much pull, but in other kinds of fishing—such as in angling for bass, pike, tarpon, snook, etc.—skillful knot tying means the difference between simply hooking fish or *hooking fish and landing them!*

There are hundreds of good knots that can be used by fishermen. And many a fisherman considers it a measure of angling skill if he is the master of several dozen different kinds of knots.

The average angler under average fishing conditions—whether he employs bait, spinning, or fly tackle—need know only a few knots. Even the most experienced fishermen, those who use different tackle under different conditions in different places, frequently utilize only a dozen or so knots, even though they know how to tie most knots of angling value. For example, probably 70 percent of the fishing situations that arise can be taken care of by the fisherman who knows how to tie a "clinch knot," a "barrel knot," a "double surgeon's knot," and a "nail knot." However, there are dozens upon dozens of different kinds of knots, *and under certain circumstances each knot is extremely valuable.* Thus the skilled angler can tie *many different knots!*

Fishermen should know that any knot will reduce the strength of fishing line to some extent; how much depends upon the knot you use and how carefully you tie it. For example, when you tie nylon line to a lure with the clinch knot, you reduce the strength of the monofilament by 10 to 15 percent. If you tie the knot carelessly, it reduces the strength of the mono even more. (Putting only five turns in a clinch knot is important because four turns decrease the knot's strength substantially. Six turns gives less strength than five, and seven are worse than six.)

The average quality knot however, when properly tied, should reduce line strength to no more than 85 percent, and the best knots will give around 95 percent of the stated line strength.

Although all knots will reduce a line's strength somewhat, there are some knots so bad they should never be used by fishermen under any circumstances. No such knots are listed in this book.

Too, it must be realized that monofilament line, when bent over on itself at certain angles, is *self cutting.* Thus knots such as the "figure eight," "half-hitch," and "double half-hitch," are *cutting knots,* and therefore should be avoided *whenever possible* by the angler.

When learning to tie a knot it is best to practice with heavy cord, light rope, or even a discarded fly line rather than with monofilament or other fishing line. The heavier material will show more clearly how the knot is shaped and formed, and once the beginner learns how to tie a knot with heavy material, he then can tie it readily with standard fishing lines.

When knots are not tied properly, the most expensive fishing tackle is useless. Even casting perfection, and stream or fish knowledge, are of no value if a knot pulls free or cuts itself when a fish strikes. So it is that every fisherman should make every effort to learn to tie knots skillfully, and it is hoped that this book will help to make that task simpler.

An attempt has been made in FISHERMEN'S KNOTS to eliminate the confusion that comes with many various names for the same knot. Some popular knots are known under a variety of names, so as many of the common names as possible are listed for each knot.

When fishing, you may want to keep this book in your tackle box, trouser, or jacket pocket so that you can quickly refer to it when some knotty angling problem arises. Too, you may find it beneficial to review certain chapters or certain knots from time to time, especially when you are faced with a new fishing experience—such as fishing for tarpon for the first time.

This is the **first** and **only** knot-tying guide allowing for easy stream, lake, ocean, or bay-side reference to the tying of *all* known knots of practical value to **all** fishermen. The nearly 150 knots in this book are useful to all anglers, regardless of whether they are still fishermen, spin fishermen, bait casters, trollers, or fly fishermen, and regardless of whether they fish in fresh water or salt, or both. Too, all the knots in this book have been proven not only scientifically via machine testing, but—and perhaps of more importance—they have been tested over many years under actual and varied fishing conditions.

It is hoped that you will find this book instructive and helpful, and that it will aid you in bringing to net or gaff many more fish, and especially those trophy fish that, otherwise, might have been just another lunker that got away.

Tom McNally
Bob McNally

1 Knotty Problems

Fishermen today have many more knot-tying problems than did fishermen years ago. The "age of synthetics" has made it necessary for all anglers to become skilled at knot tying.

In other days fishermen had lines and leaders made of "natural" materials, silk fly lines, for example, silkworm gut leaders, lines braided of linen, etc. Nowadays almost all fishing line and leader materials are made of man-made materials, chiefly platyl and nylon. Many of the knots that were completely satisfactory with the old natural material lines/leaders are totally unsatisfactory with the synthetic lines/leaders marketed today. The synthetics have finishes about as smooth as glass, so many knots tied in them slip readily, and therefore are useless.

Excluding the metal lines, most modern fishing lines are braided Dacron, braided nylon, or nylon monofilament. Dacron is a fine-diameter line with little stretch , and is used primarily in salt water trolling. Braided nylon lines are popular among anglers using revolving spool reels, in both fresh and salt water. Braided nylon is soft, spools nicely, is water repellent, and it wears well.

Monofilament is the most popular fishing line, for just about all fishing conditions. It is smooth, wears well, can be had in a variety of characteristics (amount of limpness, elasticity, resistance to abra-

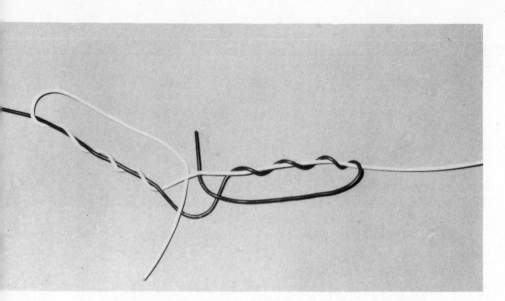

Knots should be carefully "formed" before being drawn up and tightened. This is the beginning stages of a Blood Knot.

sion, etc.), and it is **the** line to use when fishing with open-face spinning reels.

Monofilament, however, fully taxes the angler's knowledge of knots, and his ability to tie them. Nylon monofilament line (which also is the most common leader material) must be tied very carefully to be tied properly. In knots where the friction is against material other than monofilament itself, the knot will likely slip. But in knots where the friction is chiefly on the monofilament itself, there is less chance for the knot to slip, break, or untie.

Four basic steps should be taken in tying any knot correctly. The knot should be formed or "shaped," then drawn, then tightened, and finally, checked.

The first step—forming or shaping of the knot—is vital. A knot that is not formed correctly will not draw up properly, nor will it tighten as it should. Build or "form" each knot slowly and carefully, being sure each turn is turned as it should be, each loop in its proper place, and so on. After the knot has been formed satisfactorily, it should be drawn up slowly. Do not yank on the knot ends, or on the line/leader material; instead, pull the ends evenly and gently, so that all

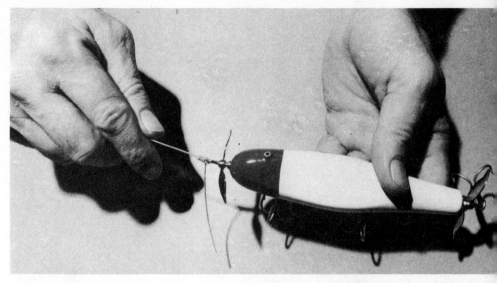

A firm, steady pull is used to tighten this Clinch Knot.

components of the knot remain in their proper places and fit together snugly. A steady, even pressure should be used in drawing up the knot.

A knot can be drawn more easily if it is wetted with saliva or with water. Both act as lubricants which help the knot components to slide smoothly into place. Also, a thumb nail can be used to push the turns of a knot together until they are seated firmly.

To tighten a knot, pull firmly and steadily on the standing parts, as well as on all ends. As much pressure should be applied as the line will take without breaking. It is not possible to tighten a knot too much. Any knot that isn't tightened correctly is going to slip under sufficient pressure, and then will either break or pull free.

It's easy to cut hands or fingers when tightening knots, especially with monofilament. And, surprisingly, the finer diameter the mono, the more readily it seems to cut. A handkerchief wrapped around the hand or fingers will prevent mono cuts, or light gloves may be worn.

Knots in heavy material can be tightened with pliers, or by wrapping the line around a sneaker and pulling it firmly with both hands. Still another way, when a knot has been tied to a fly or lure, is

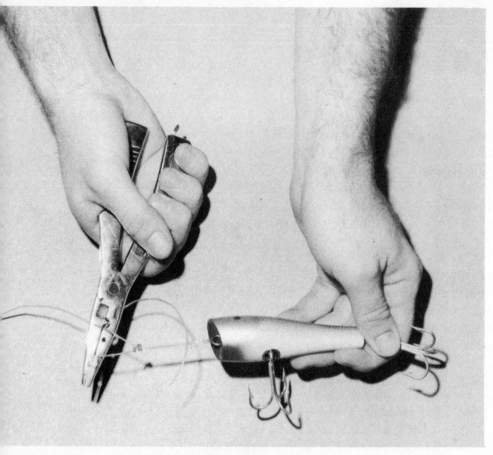

Very heavy monofilament, when knotted, calls for the use of pliers to exert sufficient pull to properly tighten all knots.

to attach a hook to a metal ring that is well seated—a screw eye, for example—and then to pull on the standing line and the knot's tag end to tighten the knot securely.

When tightening a knot that is connected to a fly or lure, be careful to keep fingers away from the hook. Many a fly fisherman, for instance, has buried a fly hook into his thumb because the fly slipped from between his thumb and index finger as he drew the knot tight. Being in a direct line with the fisherman's thumb, the fly hook had no place to go except into the thumb.

The final step in knot tying, or knot "building," is checking or testing the completed knot. No experienced angler ever ties a knot and then starts fishing; he checks a new knot carefully before making his first cast.

In checking a knot, first take a good look at it to see if it appears right. Many improperly tied knots look just that way—like improperly tied knots. If you notice that a turn hasn't pulled into place exactly right, that there is an unwanted hump in the knot, or some other deficiency, cut the knot off and tie another.

If a knot looks right, test it by pulling against it with whatever pressure the line or leader will bear. Pull on both sides of the knot, if it is a knot joining lines.

If the knot you've tied connects to a hook, fly, or lure, attach the hook, etc. to a screw eye or something similar and pull hard. If it's a different kind of knot, such as line to line, you can check it by wrapping part of the line around a sneaker and hauling on it, just as you would to tighten a heavy, strong line.

Never test a knot by a sudden jerk or yank on the line. Perfectly good lines, and perfectly good knots, can be popped by giving them sudden, powerful jolts. Neither lines nor knots are made to withstand that sort of abuse.

After completing a knot, trim its tag ends as close to the knot as possible. Many fishermen do not trim the excess tag ends of a knot closely because they fear the knot may pull out. Any knot that is properly tied can be trimmed very close and it will not pull out or loosen.

Tag ends should be **cut**, never burned with a cigarette or match. Burning can weaken the knot or the adjoining line. A sharp knife, razor, scissors, almost anything can be used to trim knots closely, but easily the best tool for this is a pair of so-called nail clippers—the kind made especially for fishermen. Heavy-duty clippers are available that will readily cut the heaviest nylon monofilament or other kinds of lines. Clippers make it possible to trim a knot very close.

Many beginners at knot tying compound their problems by never allowing themselves enough line or leader material with which to

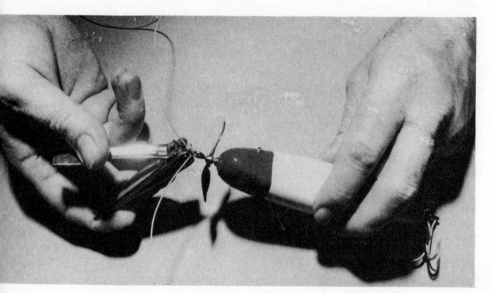

The surplus, or tag ends of finished knots, should be trimmed as close as possible. Clippers do the best job.

easily tie a knot. Fishing lines and nylon monofilament leader material are inexpensive, so there is no reason to skimp on line when tying a knot. Always allow at least eight or ten inches of line to work with when tying a knot, and some knots require more line than that if they are to be formed readily. By allowing plenty of line with which to tie a knot, the knot will draw up best and, moreover, you'll be able to tie any given knot more quickly.

Skilled anglers always check their lines or leaders before tying in a knot. The line or leader that has abrasions, nicks, or other weak spots should be discarded; the best knot tied into such a line/leader is useless, since the line/leader is going to part under the first pressure applied to it.

It's difficult to tie decent knots in monofilament that is kinked or that is "spirally." Line left on reels for very long usually will be spirally, and fly fishing leaders often are full of kinks.

The best way to straighten kinky monofilament is to run it between the folds of a rubber square, over a section of rubber hose, under tennis shoes or other rubber-soled shoes, or around the ankle of rubber boots. The friction created by the rubbing of the monofilament against the rubber will straighten the line. Be sure, however, that the shoe, boot, or whatever is free of sand or dirt; otherwise, you might cut or fray the mono.

2 Line-to-Line Knots

The need for knotting two fishing lines together is an everyday occurrence in the world of angling. Some fishermen use the proper knots for this job, but most don't.

This chapter illustrates and explains the many different knots that have been designed for the specific purpose of connecting one line to another.

One such knot is the Blood Knot. It is world famous for tying together two pieces of nylon monofilament line that are of *nearly equal diameter*. The Blood Knot is a good one, but it won't do everything. For example, it isn't an appropriate knot for tying 60-pound test mono to 12-pound test mono. Instead, a Shocker Knot should be used to join lines of such varying diameters.

Under various fishing conditions, each knot presented in this chapter is of special value to anglers at one time or another. All the known knots that serve to dependably connect fishing lines are included. This means those knots specifically designed for joining nylon monofilament, braided lines, and fly lines. (Knots for connecting fishing lines to wire are covered in Chapter 6.)

Explanations are given in this chapter on how, why, and when a particular knot should or should not be used to join a couple lines.

ANOTHER DROPPER KNOT

This is a fine knot for tying a dropper line to a leader or other line when an Extension Blood Knot isn't practical. When the Dropper Knot is "jammed" against a knot in the leader or line, as shown, it makes a small connection that readily runs through rod guides.

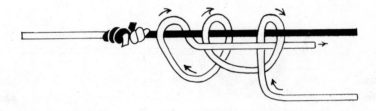

Fig. 1 Lay the leader or line, and the dropper line, side by side. Wrap the dropper line around the leader three times, then push the end of the dropper back through the first loop.

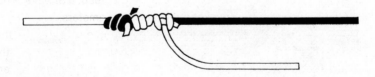

Fig. 2 Pull the knot tight, trim its ends, and the finished knot will look like this.

LEADER KNOT (Sometimes called Knot Canada)

This knot is an excellent one for tying two nylon lines together, and some experts feel it's much easier to tie than the Blood Knot.

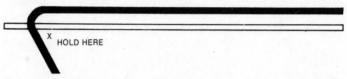

Fig. 1 Lap the ends of the strands as shown, holding with thumb and forefinger where marked.

Fig. 2 Loop end around both lines and poke end through all three loops.

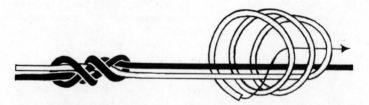

Fig. 3 Now twist the other end around both strands three times and stick end through all three loops.

Fig. 4 When both sides of knot look like this, slowly pull the knot tight and use your fingernails to push the loops together.

Fig. 5 Finished knot looks like this. Trim ends close to knot.

FISHERMAN'S BEND KNOT

This is an excellent knot for joining two lines of equal diameter. However, it is difficult to tie and other knots, such as the Blood Knot, are more often used by knowledgeable anglers.

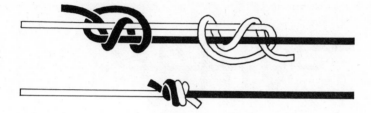

VARIATION OF FISHERMAN'S BEND

Some anglers still use this variation because the ends of the knot are in the center, and the knot passes through rod guides easily. Although it's much easier to tie this knot than the regular Fisherman's Bend, there are many other knots for joining lines of equal diameter that can be tied much more quickly.

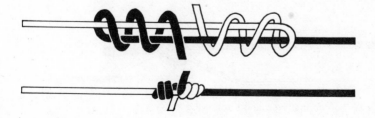

MULTIPLE CLINCH KNOT

This is the ideal knot for bait casters who use nylon leaders six or eight feet long, because they need a knot joining leader to line that isn't bulky. This knot passes from reel through rod guides easily, and is extremely strong.

SHOCKER KNOT

This is a good knot for tying two lines of different diameters together. It's easy and fast to tie, yet strong and secure.

(For more information on this knot, turn to page 171.)

Fig. 1 Make an Overhand Knot in the light line. Form a loose Overhand Knot in the heavy line and pass the end of the light line through the Overhand Knot.

Fig. 2 Tighten the Overhand Knot in the heavy line.

Fig. 3 Make three wraps with the light line around the heavy line, and pass the
end back through the first loop.

THE ANGLER'S KNOT (Also called Single Fishermen's Knot)

This is an excellent, quickly-tied knot for tying a dropper line to a
leader. It's very popular with fly fishermen, however more and more
anglers, other than fly fishermen, are using dropper lines so they can
fish two or more flies, or lures, at the same time. The Angler's Knot is
simple to tie; just make two Overhand Knots, each around the
standing part of the other line.
(For more information on this knot, turn to page 153.)

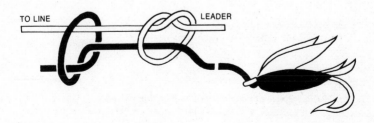

TO LINE   LEADER

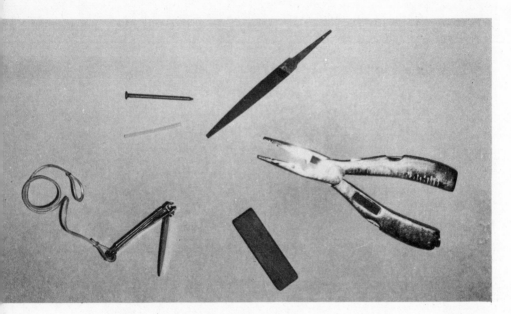

Handy tools for every knot tier include light file and hone for sharpening hooks, pliers for pulling heavy knots tight, nail and/or tube for tying nail knots, and clippers for trimming knots.

VARIATION OF THE NAIL KNOT

This knot was only recently developed. It's best used when tying a heavy leader butt to a fly line. Because there are only a few wraps, some anglers feel this knot is easier to tie than a conventional Nail Knot. However, some other Nail Knots, such as the Fast Nail Knot, are even easier to tie than this one, and moreover, are stronger. Thus this Nail Knot should be used only by fishermen who have difficulty tying the other types.

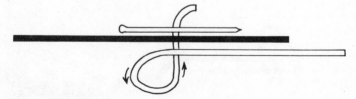

Fig. 1 No tying is done with the fly line. Hold the nail parallel to the fly line and form a loop with the leader butt.

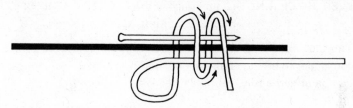

Fig. 2 Hold the loop below the fly line and wrap the leader's butt end twice around the fly line, nail, and standing part of the leader.

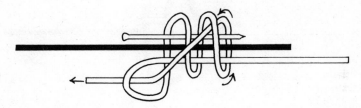

Fig. 3 Put the butt end through the last wrap and the first loop, as shown.

Fig. 4 Push all the wraps tightly together with your thumb nail, and withdraw the nail slowly.

Fig. 5 Pull on both ends of the leader, then trim the leader and line tag ends.

TILLER HITCH KNOT (Commonly known as Tiller Knot, Slipped Hitch, Hitch Knot, and Helm Knot)

This old and reliable sailor's knot is a very good one for fastening a nylon leader to braided bait-casting line. This knot is useful because it can be untied easily, yet holds well when pulled tight.

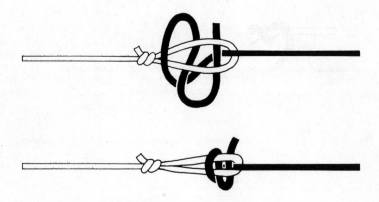

EXTENSION BLOOD KNOT

This knot is primarily used by fly fishermen who want to fish two flies simultaneously. It achieves the same results as all of the so-called "dropper knots," yet it is much stronger. A normal Blood Knot is tied and only one of the leader ends is trimmed. The dropper fly is tied to the untrimmed leader end. (For more information on this knot, turn to page 151.)

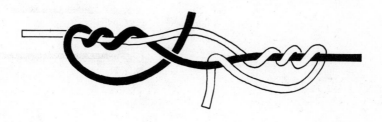

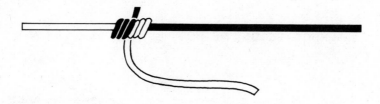

JAM KNOT (also called Pinch Jam)

All of these "Jam Knots" are used chiefly for joining a fly line to a leader. They are very practical knots for joining almost any kind of lines, but the fisherman must be careful to tie the Overhand Knot very well before pulling the "Jam Knot" tight.

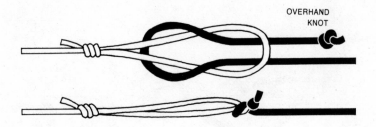

OVERHAND
KNOT

JAM KNOT—SECOND METHOD (also known as Jam Hitch)

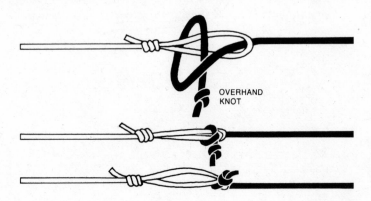

OVERHAND
KNOT

JAM KNOT—THIRD METHOD

SURGEON'S KNOT (Occasionally called the Double Water Knot and
Joiner Knot)

Many skilled anglers consider this the best knot for joining two
lines of greatly varying diameters. It is primarily used by fly fishermen
and other anglers who need a "shock leader" when after toothy fish
such as northern pike, or fish with sharp gill plates, such as tarpon
and snook.

The Surgeon's Knot can be difficult to tighten. It's best to moisten
the knot, then pull *all four loose ends* of the knot slowly and evenly
until tight. (For more information on this knot, turn to page 158.)

SHOCK LEADER

TO REEL

TYING A NAIL KNOT USING LINE LOOP INSTEAD OF NAIL

This is an ordinary Nail Knot but no nail or tube is needed to tie it. This method of tying a Nail Knot is useful when nails, tubes, etc., are not available.

Fig. 1 Cut a short piece of line, double it over and lay alongside the fly line. Make six turns with leader end, and bring through loop in short piece of line.

Fig. 2 Pull short line through loops of knot, which will bring leader end with it, as shown.

Fig. 3 Pull tightly on both ends of leader to tighten knot.

Fig. 4 Trim the short end of fly line and leader.

FIGURE EIGHT KNOT

This knot is occasionally used in emergency situations to join a leader to a line. The knot is easy to tie and untie, however it has a low breaking strength and should *only* be used when it is not practical to tie a better knot, such as a Nail Knot or a Surgeon's Knot. (For more information on this knot, turn to page 195.)

KNOT FOR ATTACHING LEADER TO LINE

This knot is popular among fishermen who find it difficult to tie the Nail Knot, yet want a knot that will go through rod guides easily. The knot takes some practice, but is actually easy to tie and is very strong.

Fig. 1 Lay the line and leader side by side. Wrap one line around the other strand twice, then poke the end around back through the two loops. Follow the same procedure when tying the second knot.

Fig. 2 When the two loose ends have been trimmed, the finished knot looks like this. Tied properly, the knot will pass through rod guides well.

TUCKED SHEET BEND KNOT

This is a safe and easy knot to tie for joining a leader to a line. The advantage of this knot is that it can be readily tied with any kind of line.

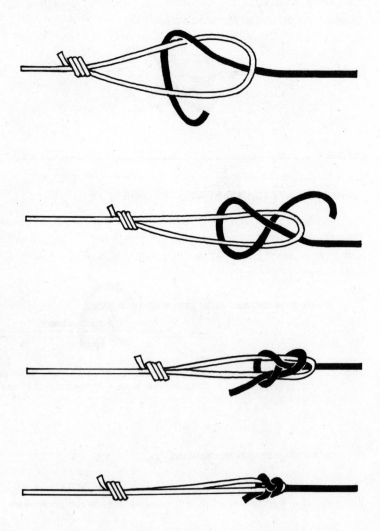

Chunky three pound brown trout is angler's reward for tying good knots.

LEADER DROPPER LOOP

This is a unique way to tie a dropper loop. Simply loop one end of monofilament leader, lay it next to the other leader strand, and then tie a simple Overhand Knot, leaving a large loop to which a dropper strand may be readily tied.

The Leader Dropper Loop should only be used sparingly, since the Extension Blood Knot is stronger and better.

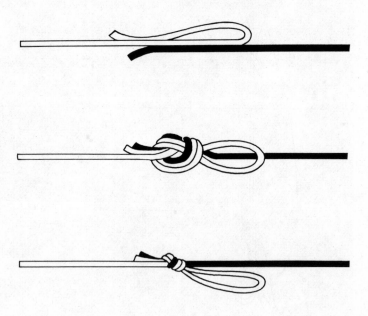

DROPPER SNELL KNOT

This knot is used for tying dropper snells to a leader. The dropper line loop is held next to the leader, then the line end is put back through the loop and pulled tight.

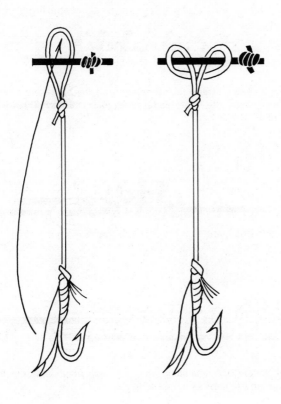

DOUBLE NAIL KNOT

This knot is important to fly fishermen because it is less bulky and easier to form than a Blood Knot when tying leaders of heavy monofilament. As with a Blood Knot, the two leader strands to be joined *must* be of nearly equal diameter for the knot to hold well.

Fig. 1 Wrap one leader strand four times around the other and around the nail, then pass the first leader end back through the loops, as illustrated.

Fig. 2 Remove the nail, and pull the first knot partially tight.

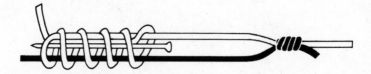

Fig. 3 Tie the second knot the same way, as shown, again withdraw the nail, and tighten the knot as done before.

Fig. 4 Push both knots together so they "jam," then tighten securely.

OVERHAND DROPPER TIE KNOT

This is a quick way of tying in a dropper line. The knot is simple to tie, but should be used only when more time cannot be used to tie another, better knot. (For more information on this knot, turn to page 166.)

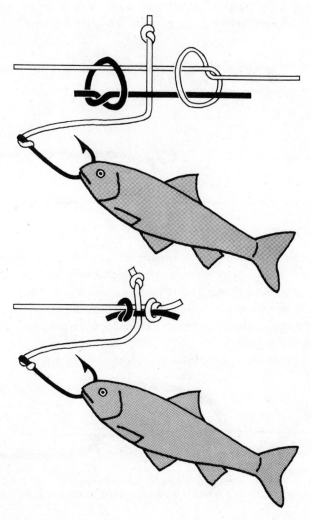

BARREL KNOT

Although this is one of the best knots for joining lines of similar diameter, it's one of the most difficult to tie. The advantage of the Barrel Knot is that it is small, goes through rod guides with ease, and is very strong. Heavy monofilament or a fly line should be used when practicing tying this knot. With heavy mono or fly line it is easier to "form" and work the knot into place as it's being tightened.

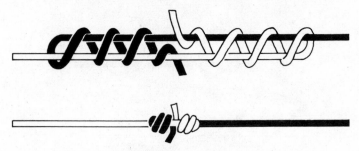

BLOOD KNOT

This knot is valuable to all fishermen, particularly fly fishermen who use it to join nylon strands in making tapered leaders. Its only drawback is that the nylon strands to be connected must be of equal, or nearly equal, diameter. The Blood Knot provides a small connection, and when properly tied it cannot pull loose no matter how close its ends are clipped.

(For more information on this knot, turn to page 156.)

Fig. 1 Cross the two lines, and wrap one line three times around the other. Now place the end through the loop formed by the two lines.

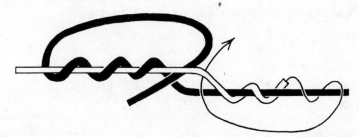

Fig. 2 Turn the other line around the standing part of the first three times, and put its free end through the loop from the opposite side.

Fig. 3 The turns should look like this. Now slowly pull on both long ends of the lines.

Fig. 4 The finished knot looks like this, with its loose ends trimmed closely.

NAIL KNOT (Sometimes referred to as Tube Knot)

This knot is used to join a large diameter line to a small diameter line, as when tying a shock tippet to a leader; it will connect heavy sections of leader material without forming a bulky knot; and it can be used to tie monofilament line to a fly line. Although a nail was originally used in tying this famous knot, many anglers use a small tube, ice pick, piece of coat hanger, or an air-pump needle. It doesn't matter what is used, so long as its surface is smooth so the monofilament slides off the tool easily.

(For more information on this knot, turn to page 164.)

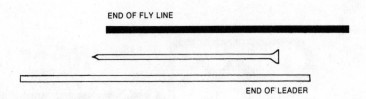

Fig. 1 Lay out the fly line and leader with the nail or tube in between, as shown in the illustration.

Fig. 2 Wrap the leader back toward the end of the fly line, making five tight turns. Then pass the free end back through the center of the loops.

Fig. 3 This is how the knot should now look, with the nail or tube still in place.

Fig. 4 Pull on both ends of the leader, and slowly withdraw the nail or tube.

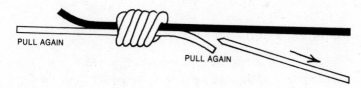

Fig. 5 Once the nail is removed, pull tightly on all four strands of line protruding from the knot.

Fig. 6 This is how the finished knot looks, with the two short ends trimmed close.

TRIPLE FISHERMAN'S KNOT

This is just an improved version of the Fisherman's Knot. It is used for joining two strands of nylon monofilament and is a good knot for making fly leaders. Although it does take some practice to tie it properly, it is a superb connection. (For more information on this knot, turn to page 159.)

EMERGENCY DROPPER KNOT

This is a fast, strong knot for tying dropper snells to a leader. This knot should only be used when it is impossible to tie the Extension Blood Knot, however. The Extension Blood Knot is a much more secure tie for droppers.

IMPROVED BLOOD KNOT

This is a superb knot for joining two lines of different diameters—for example, tying 12-pound test line to 80-pound test line.

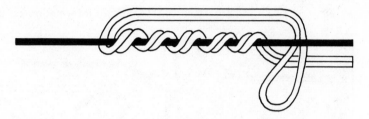

Fig. 1 Double the smaller diameter line. Wrap it five times around the larger diameter line and bring it back between the two strands.

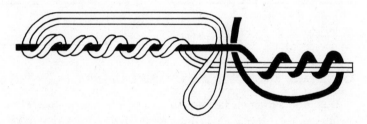

Fig. 2 Twist the larger diameter line around the doubled line three times, and place its free end back through the loop in the opposite direction.

Fig. 3 Pull the knot slowly to tighten it. Use your fingernails to push the loops of the knot together. Trim all loose ends one-fourth inch from the knot.

DOUBLE BECKET BEND KNOT

Although this is not the best knot for tying a line to a leader loop, it is quick and easy to tie. In an emergency it can be of practical value to the angler.

OVERHAND KNOT WITH A KNOTTED END

This is an extremely fast way to tie a fly line or other heavy line to a leader's loop. However, it is not a particularly strong knot because it employs an Overhand Knot which tends to cut itself under extreme pressure.

To tie this knot, first put an Overhand Knot in the end of the fly line. Next pass the fly line through the leader loop, then tie another Overhand Knot in the fly line.

JOINING TWO LOOPS

Although not the best way, this is one of the most popular methods of joining a fly line and leader, or of joining braided line to monofilament line. If the two lines are tightened correctly, as shown in figure two, they will form a secure connection.

(For more information on this knot, turn to page 147.)

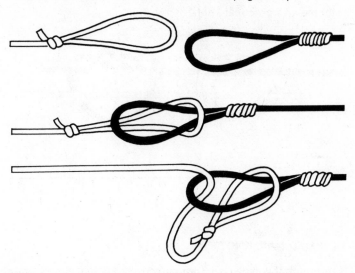

Fig. 1 Pass one loop through the "eye" of the other loop. Then pull the remaining line through the loop, as shown.

Fig. 2 When the two loops are drawn tight they should look like this.

WOLF KNOT (Often referred to as Wolf Splice)

This knot originated in Germany, and for years it was the "bread-and-butter" tie for connecting silkworm gut and synthetic leaders. Although gut leaders have generally been replaced by nylon monofilament leaders, the Wolf Knot is still a good, secure tie to use, even with nylon. This knot is overlooked by most anglers, yet it is a valuable and practical knot.

MODIFIED NAIL KNOT

Although this type Nail Knot can be used to join almost any kind of lines, it was originally designed for connecting lead-core trolling line to monofilament line. Too, fly rodders use the Modified Nail Knot for joining lead-core fly lines to leaders and backing.

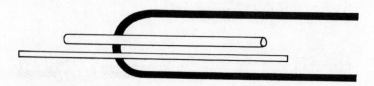

Fig. 1 Lay two lines next to each other, alongside a plastic or metal tube, just as you would if tying a standard Nail Knot.

Fig. 2 Wind one line around the tube, as well as around the second line.

Fig. 3 After three wraps with the first line, take *both* lines and wind them once around the tube.

Fig. 4 Then continue wrapping with the first line, as shown in the illustration.

Fig. 5 Next pass the first line back through the tube, pull the lines snug, slip the tube out, and tighten the knot.

Fig. 6 This is how the completed knot looks.

PENDRE DROPPER KNOT

The Pendre Knot is a good one for tying nylon dropper lines to leaders. This knot is used often by experienced fly fishermen, and it was originated in Switzerland.

(For more information on this knot, turn to page 152.)

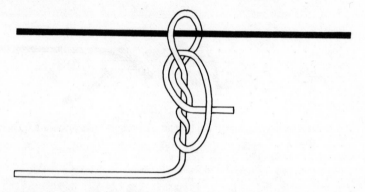

Fig. 1 Wrap the dropper line around the leader. Make three turns around the standing part of the dropper line with the end of the dropper line, then pass the end through the first and last loops, as shown in the illustration.

OFFSET NAIL KNOT

Although this is an elaborate and difficult knot to tie, it is one of the best for joining two strands of monofilament line having different diameters. The knot is used chiefly by fly anglers who use fast tapered leaders. Some fly fishermen prefer this knot over the Surgeon's Knot because the Offset Nail Knot goes through rod guides easier.

Fig. 1 Wind the heavy line twice around the lighter line and the nail. Then push the heavy line end back through the center, as illustrated. Remove the nail and partially tighten the knot.

Fig. 2 Wrap the lighter test line eight times around the heavier test line and the nail, then push the end of the lighter test line back through the loops.

Fig. 3 Remove the nail and slowly pull all four of the ends tight.

Fig. 4 This is how the finished knot looks.

VARIATION OF THE ANGLER'S KNOT

This connection is simply a regular Angler's Knot carried one step farther. The extra tie in the knot makes it more secure than an ordinary Angler's Knot.

This Variation of the Angler's Knot is used primarily for tying a dropper line to monofilament leaders.

SINGLE WATER KNOT

The Single Water Knot is a simple Overhand Knot using both lines for the tie. It is not as secure as some knots, such as the Surgeon's Knot, when used to connect two pieces of monofilament. However, the Single Water Knot is fast and easy to tie.

DOUBLE WATER LOOP KNOT (Sometimes called Double Fisherman's Knot)

This knot was orginally designed for tying gut leaders, however, some skilled anglers still use the knot to join monofilament lines. The Double Water Loop Knot seems complicated, but it can be tied quickly and easily with practice.

FAST NAIL KNOT (Occasionally called Speed Nail Knot and 20-Second Nail Knot)

Many anglers do not use the Nail Knot because ordinarily tying it is difficult and time consuming. However, the Fast Nail Knot is one of the easiest, quickest, and most secure knots for joining two lines of nearly equal diameter. The knot is most commonly used for joining the butt end of a fly leader to a fly line.

No special "tool" is needed to tie this knot. A nail, paper clip, match stick, toothpick, or any other stiff, small diameter object may be used.

This knot is the same as "Snelling A Hook," so if you practice "snelling," tying the Fast Nail Knot will be much easier for you. (For more information on this knot, turn to page 160–62.)

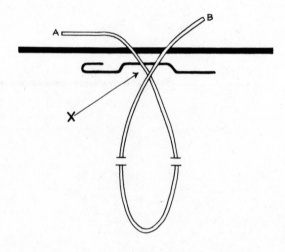

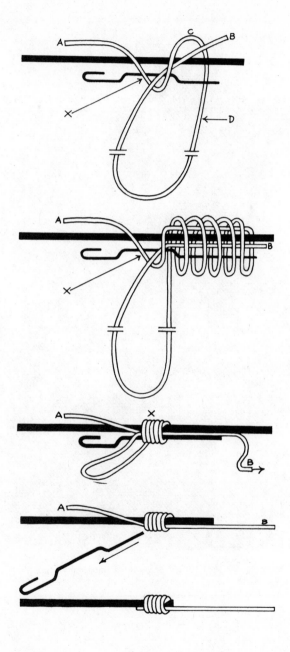

Ed Curnow, guide and tackle shop proprietor at Ennis, Montana, ties an Instant Nail Knot.

SNAKE DROPPER KNOT

This is a strong knot for tying a nylon dropper line to a leader or line. It's an extremely popular knot in Europe.

Fig. 1 Place the dropper line beside the standing line. Make a loop in the dropper, and put its long end through the loop. Now make two turns, going around both the dropper line and the other strand.

FISHING LINE

DROPPER LINE

Fig. 2 Pull both ends of the dropper line to tighten the knot, then trim short end close to knot. Finished knot should appear as illustrated.

ALBRIGHT SPECIAL KNOT (Also known as Key Knot Splice and Key Loop)

This is an excellent knot for tying light monofilament to heavy monofilament line, wire cable, nylon-coated wire, and even to small diameter single-strand wire leader.

Although it takes time to learn to tie the Albright Special well, this is a very useful and strong knot that passes through rod guides with ease.

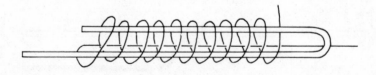

COMPOSITE KNOT

This is a half Water Knot and half Jam Knot. It's used for tying heavy nylon "shock tippets" to light nylon when fishing for species such as tarpon and northern pike.

Fig. 1 Make a loose Overhand Knot with the heavy line. Pass the short end of the light line through the Overhand Knot and wrap six times around the heavy line.

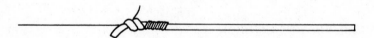

Fig. 2 Tighten the Overhand Knot in the heavy line first, then slowly pull knot tight. Clip the loose ends close to the knot.

SQUARE KNOT (Also known as Reef Knot)

This is a commonly used boating knot. It is a fast, efficient means to join two lines that are of equal diameter.

The knot is very reliable when all line ends are tied securely, and when there is equal tension on both lines.

NAIL KNOT USING HOOK

This is a very practical and easy way to tie a Nail Knot. It can "save the day" for those anglers who forget to bring tubes or other "tools" with which to tie Nail Knots while fishing.

The trick in tying this knot is to keep the leader loops very loose until the hook eye and leader end are pulled through the loops. The knot is then pulled tight and the leader end trimmed close.

ANOTHER IMPROVED BLOOD KNOT

This version of the Blood Knot is somewhat bulkier than the original Blook Knot. However, it is easy to tie and is one of the best connections for joining monofilament line. It is extremely important to form and tighten this knot well for it to have the best possible strength.

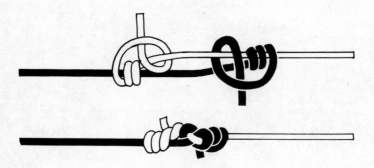

WATER KNOT

This is a popular knot among bait casters for tying breaks in braided line. This knot is occasionally used for tying nylon monofilament, but it's not as good as some knots like the Blood Knot.

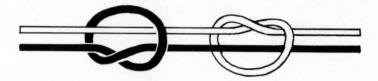

Fig. 1 Tie two Overhand Knots, each around the standing end of the other line.

Fig. 2 To improve the knot make several wraps around the standing part of each line, and poke the ends back through the loops.

3 Knots For Tying Lines To Hooks, Lures, Swivels, etc.

This chapter of FISHERMEN'S KNOTS is of special importance to *all* fishermen. Regardless of what kind of fishing is being done, with what kind of tackle, or where the fishing is being done, the angler must join his fishing line to some sort of connecting ring. He may be tying his line directly to the "eye" or ring of a hook, or to the ring of a lure or swivel, and so on. But whatever, he will have need for one or more of the knots presented in this chapter.

The knots tied to connecting rings most often are the ones that break or pull out when fighting hooked fish. Thus the knot joining the fishing line or leader to the lure, swivel, etc. is one of the most important in any knots system. Therefore, it should be tied carefully and deliberately.

Some special purpose knots are included in this chapter, but most of the following knots are applicable to everyday fishing problems. Moreover, it pays to be able to tie a variety of knots for connecting line to hooks, lures, and so on.

For example, an Improved Clinch Knot normally is adequate for joining fishing line to lure or hook. However, if very heavy monofilament line is being used, it will be almost impossible to tie an Improved Clinch Knot, since the heavy mono resists being pulled up tightly. The knot to use in such a situation would be the Palomar Knot, which is easy to tie with even the heaviest monofilament.

DOUBLE IMPROVED CLINCH KNOT

Fig. 1 Double the line, bringing the line end back parallel to the standing line so there is about eight inches of double line. Take the end of the double line and push it through the hook eye. Wrap the doubled line end five times around the doubled standing part of the line, and push the line end back through the loop formed near the hook eye.

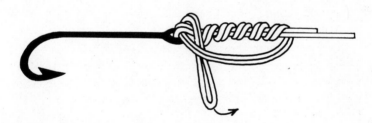

Fig. 2 Pull the doubled line end through the loop in front of the hook eye, then push the end through the large loop, as shown.

Fig. 3 Moisten the knot with saliva, then pull tight.

DOUBLE IMPROVED CLINCH KNOT (continued)

The Double Improved Clinch Knot is an extremely secure tie. However, it is difficult to tie with heavy monofilament and with braided lines. Thus the knot is not practical when after fish for which a heavy leader or line is necessary. For that reason the Double Improved Clinch Knot is used most often by fresh water anglers after such species as largemouth and smallmouth bass, panfish, and trout.

DOUBLE TURLE KNOT

This is merely a standard Turle Knot carried one step farther. Instead of making a single wrap with the Overhand Knot, as when tying the standard Turle Knot, two wraps are made with the line end around the standing part of the line before passing the hook back through the loop.

The regular Turle Knot originally was designed for tying gut leaders to hooks with turned-up or turned-down eyes. The Double Turle Knot, however, was created for use with nylon monofilament lines. It is stronger and more dependable than the Turle Knot.

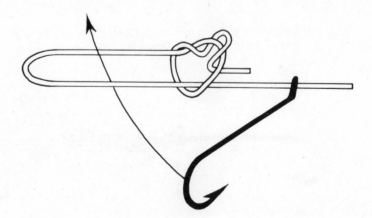

DUNCAN LOOP KNOT

Here is an excellent "sliding loop" knot. When the knot is tied, it can be tightened anywhere on the standing part of the line, which means an angler can adjust the knot to form any size loop he desires. The loop will remain open during normal casting and retrieving. However, when a fish is hooked, the knot will slide down the line and "jam" tightly against the hook eye. After the fish is landed the knot can be moved up the line and the loop opened once again.

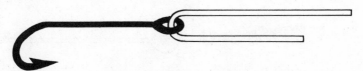

Fig. 1 Put the line end through the hook eye, bringing about eight inches of line through the "eye" with which to tie the knot. Keep the line end parallel to the standing line.

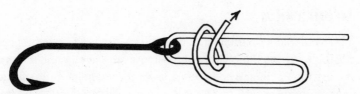

Fig. 2 Turn the line end down, so that it comes back underneath the two parallel strands. Wind the line end around the two parallel lines and through the loop, as shown.

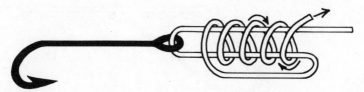

Fig. 3 Make five wraps around the two parallel lines, inside the loop. Then pull the tag end and standing part of the line to tighten the knot.

DOUBLE-O KNOT (Often called Eye Knot)

The Double-O Knot can be tied in a few moments, and it is a good knot to use with nylon monofilament, braided line, and even with nylon-coated wire.

This knot is primarily used by anglers who want a knot that can be tied quickly to ringed "eye" hooks and swivels. Thus it is popular with bait casters and spin fishermen.

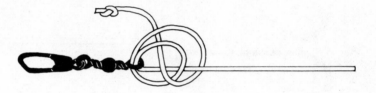

PALOMAR KNOT

Many anglers, particularly those with failing eyesight, find it difficult to tie the Clinch Knot or the Improved Clinch Knot. For those anglers the Palomar Knot is the answer for tying line or leader to a hook, lure, or swivel "eye." This is a strong, yet easy-to-tie knot. Some skilled anglers can even tie the Palomar Knot in complete darkness, using only their sense of "feel."

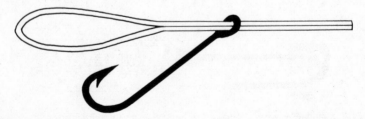

Fig. 1 Double the end of the line and pass the loop through the hook eye.

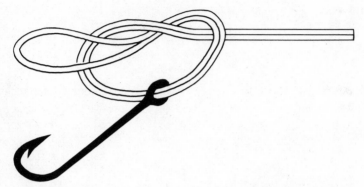

Fig. 2 Double the loop back, then make an Overhand Knot around the standing line, leaving a loop large enough for the hook (or lure) to pass back through.

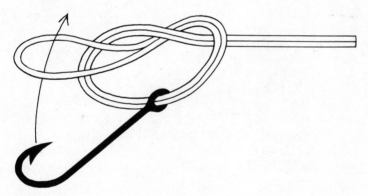

Fig. 3 Put the entire hook (lure) through the loop, as illustrated.

Fig. 4 Pulling on the standing line will draw the knot tight. Trim it, and the knot will be compact and effective.

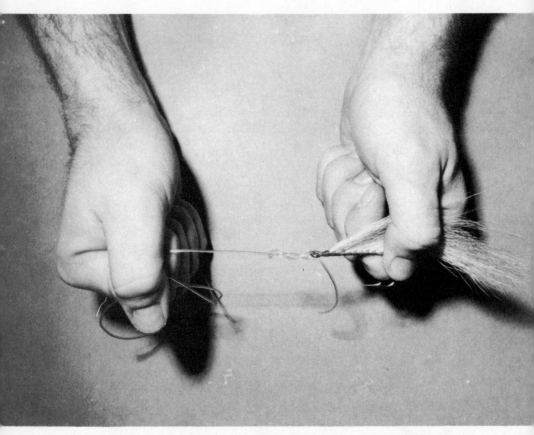

A slip when drawing knots tight can result in a hook imbedded in fingers or hand. This is a safe way to hold a hook when tightening a knot.

SERRURE KNOT

This knot looks much like several other knots, such as the Salmon Hook Knot and the Bumper Tie Knot. However, it is completely different and, moreover, it can be made with much heavier line.

The Serrure Knot was developed in France for tying nylon monofilament to "flat-eye" hooks, and it has become popular throughout Europe. The knot seems impossible to tie the first time, but with practice it becomes quite easy.

Thread the end of the line through the hook eye, pulling about six inches of line through the "eye." Now lay the line that has been pulled through the hook eye parallel to the hook shank with your thumb and index finger, and bring the line end back toward the hook eye.

Now wrap the line end four times around the line and the hook shank, back towards the bend of the hook. Push the line end through the loop that the thumb and forefinger hold. Slowly pull on the standing part of the line in front of the hook eye, until the loop that the line end was put through is pulled tight and the knot "jams" behind the hook eye.

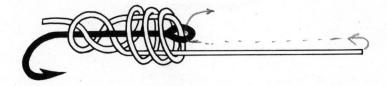

BUMPER TIE KNOT

The Bumper Tie is becoming increasingly popular with anglers who snell their own hooks. The Bumper Tie is a more complicated knot to tie than the "Snelling A Hook" Knot, or the "Quick Snell Knot." However, some fishermen prefer the Bumper Tie when using natural baits for fish such as steelhead and Chinook salmon; they feel the Bumper Tie is a stronger knot.

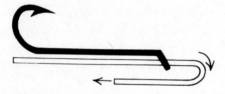

Fig. 1 The leader end is pushed through the hook eye.

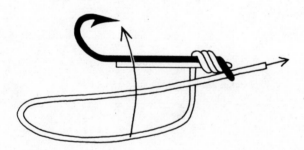

Fig. 2 The standing part of the leader is wound three times around the hook shank and the leader end. Then the *butt* end of the leader is pushed out through the hook eye.

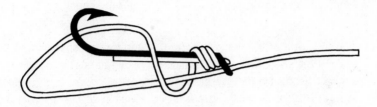

Fig. 3 A loop of about four inches is left under the hook shank, and then is wrapped around the hook shank.

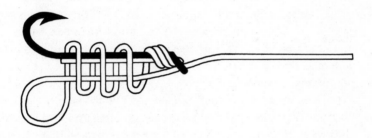

Fig. 4 The loop is wrapped around the hook shank three times, forming a series of coils.

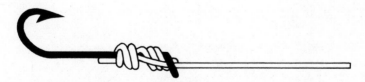

Fig. 5 Now the standing part of the leader is slowly pulled tight, and the knot is completed.

PORTLAND CREEK HITCH KNOT (Commonly called Riffling Hitch
or Newfoundland Hitch)

This is one of the most important knots for fly fishermen.

The Portland Creek Hitch is used often by Atlantic salmon anglers,
as well as by trout fishermen who want to "skim" a fly over the
surface. This knot makes the leader draw away from the head of the
fly at a 45 degree angle, causing the fly to "swim" and make a "V"
wake on the surface. Such action can be irresistible to salmon and
trout.

When a fish strikes the fly, the "hitch" slips off the fly's head
without knotting the leader.

Tying this knot properly is very important in determining the way
the fly will "work" in the water. Al McClane (the distinguished,
world-renown angler and Executive Editor of *Field & Stream Magazine*) once noted that some guides in Europe spend as much as an
hour and a half tying and re-tying the Portland Creek Hitch, and then
watching the fly in the water to see that it has the correct action
before going salmon fishing.

The Portland Hitch Knot can be used with certain streamers,
"hopper" imitations, and some dry fly patterns. The flies look more
alive when skipped or skimmed across the surface with the Portland
Hitch, and often many kinds of fish want a fly that is activated on the
surface that way.

Fig. 1 Tie the leader to the fly with a Turle Knot, then tie a Half-Hitch in the leader and pull it over the fly's head.

Fig. 2 Tighten the Half-Hitch behind the fly's head, so that the leader comes away at the bottom or side of the fly's head.

HOMER RHODE LOOP KNOT (Sometimes called Flemish Loop or Loop Knot)

This is an easy knot to tie, and very popular among salt water and Great Lakes anglers who do considerable trolling. The Homer Rhode Loop makes the use of "snap-swivels" unnecessary, and allows lures to have more "action."

The knot forms a loop through the "eye" of a lure, so the lure "swims" more freely than if a knot were tied tightly to it.

Although this knot is normally tied with monofilament line or nylon-coated wire, it also can be used effectively with braided lines.

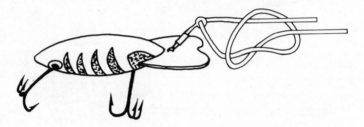

Fig. 1 Tie a simple Overhand Knot about four inches from the end of the line. Push the end of the line through the hook eye, then back through the center of the Overhand Knot.

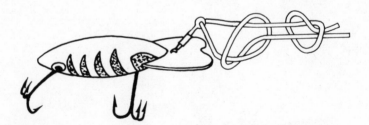

Fig. 2 Next, with the end of the line, make another Overhand Knot around the standing part of the line. Now slowly pull the two knots tight, at the same time sliding them together so they "jam" or lock against one another.

WYSS TURLE KNOT

This is an ordinary Turle Knot, with an extra step before the knot is pulled tight. Many fishermen use the Wyss Turle Knot rather than the regular Turle Knot because the Wyss Turle Knot is less likely to slip and break from pressure exerted by strong fish.

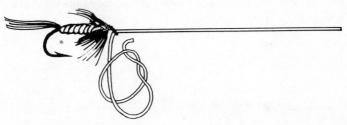

Fig. 1 Thread the leader through the hook eye. Bring the end of the leader back and tie an Overhand Knot around the standing part of the leader.

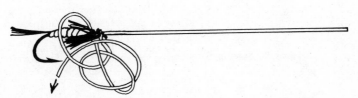

Fig. 2 Slip the loop formed by the Overhand Knot over the hook shank, and bring the end of the leader through the loop that's now around the hook shank.

Fig. 3 Hold the tag end of the leader against the hook shank, and slowly pull on the standing part of the leader to tighten the knot.

DOUBLE-LOOP CLINCH KNOT (Occasionally called Double Jam Knot)

Few anglers are aware of this fine version of the standard Clinch Knot. The Double-Loop Clinch Knot is somewhat new, and has only recently become popular among trolling fishermen.

The Double-Loop Clinch Knot is used chiefly for tying on various types of swivels when trolling. The knot takes a little more time to tie, so it is most practical when using the same terminal tackle over a long period, as is normally done when trolling.

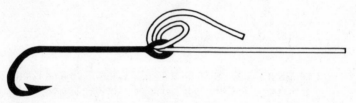

Fig. 1 Turn the line end through the hook eye twice.

Fig. 2 Wrap the line end around the standing part of the line three times, then put the line end back through the two loops in front of the hook eye.

Fig. 3 The finished knot pulled tight.

Heavy shock tippets, tied with special knots, are a "must" when fishing for toothy species such as northern pike, barracuda, etc.

SINGLE SHEET BEND KNOT

For most angling situations this knot is *not* recommended.

However, it is suitable for taking panfish, and is occasionally used by anglers employing heavy monofilament because the knot is easy to form with heavy line.

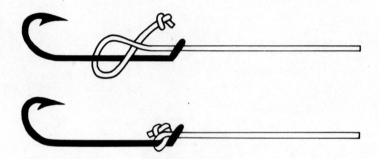

COMPOUND KNOT

Practice is the key to making the Compound Knot. It is always a difficult knot to tie, and especially for anglers who are "all thumbs."

However, the Compound Knot is a great knot for making a loop so that a lure or fly will "swim" more freely when retrieved.

The Compound Knot is a secure tie with either nylon monofilament or braided lines. It is most difficult to tie with lines testing over 50 pounds.

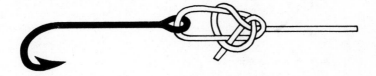

Fig. 1 Make a loose Overhand Knot about five inches from the end of the line (or leader). Pass the end of the line through the hook eye, then back through the center of the loose Overhand Knot. Wrap the line end over the standing part of the line just above the Overhand Knot, and push the line end between the two lines forming the Overhand Knot. Then go through the two lines at the top of the Overhand Knot, as shown. Slowly pull the standing part of the line, the line end, and the hook or lure to tighten the knot.

DOUBLE-LINE HALF-HITCHES KNOT

This knot is used often by salt water anglers who need a simple tie for connecting heavy monofilament line to a hook, lure, or swivel "eye." The Double-Line Half-Hitches, when tied properly and carefully, is adequate for light "inshore" salt water fishing when a shock tippet is desired.

Fig. 1 Double the end of the line, so there's about six inches of doubled line with which to tie the knot. Pass the doubled line through the hook or swivel "eye" twice. Tie two Half-Hitches with the end around the standing part of the doubled line.

Fig. 2 This is the completed, tightened Double-Line Half-Hitches.

THE END-LOOP KNOT (Sometimes called the Buffer Loop)

This is a good "loop knot" for anglers who use heavy test "shock tippets." It forms a loop with heavy mono much easier than other knots.

The End-Loop Knot is not recommended, however, for use with light lines since it weakens the line more than do some other "loop knots," such as the Nail Loop.

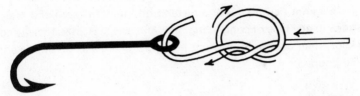

Fig. 1 Tie an Overhand Knot about six inches from the end of the line, then pass the line through the hook eye.

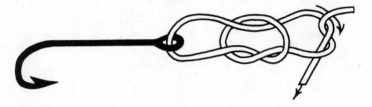

Fig. 2 Put the line end through the open Overhand Knot and tie a Half-Hitch with the line end onto the standing part of the line.

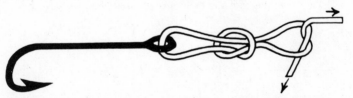

Fig. 3 Now slide the Overhand Knot either up or down the standing part of the line. This will determine the size of the loop that the knot will form. Slowly pull the line's end and its standing part to tighten the knot.

Fig. 4 Trim the knot, leaving a tag end about one-eighth-inch long.

BOW KNOT

The Bow Knot is simple and can be tied rapidly. Although it doesn't look like a secure knot, it is quite strong and reliable.

This knot can be used to fasten both monofilament and braided lines to any type of connecting ring. And, too, it is an especially good knot when used with medium-heavy nylon lines testing up to about 60 pounds.

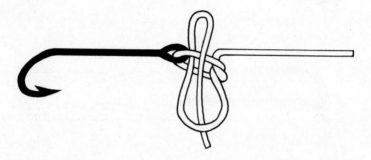

Fig. 1 The hook eye is threaded with the line end and a loose Overhand Knot is tied. Now the line end is passed through the Overhand Knot, brought back over the knot and then pushed through the loop, as illustrated.

ROUND-TURN FISHHOOK TIE

This knot is often used by anglers using heavy nylon while fishing natural baits. The knot holds best with stiff, heavy nylon rather than with wispy monofilament or braided line.

Too, the Round-Turn Fishhook Tie is a better connection when there is a constant pull or pressure from the standing part of the line to the knot, as when trolling or stillfishing.

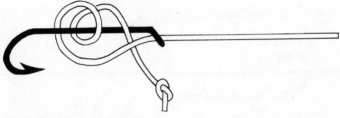

Fig. 1 Thread the line through the hook eye. Make a wrap around the shank of the hook toward the hook eye, then tuck the line end under the wrap. Now tie an Overhand Knot in the end of the line.

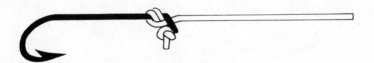

Fig. 2 Pull on the standing part of the line to tighten the knot.

SNELLING A HOOK (Commonly called Salmon Hook Knot)

Originally, Snelling A Hook was necessary because many hooks did not have "eyes." However, some expert anglers still insist today on snelling their "eyed" hooks because they feel snelling makes a strong, permanent connection.

Snelled hooks usually are used in fishing natural baits, especially for fish such as coho and Chinook salmon, and steelhead trout.

Most bait fishermen prefer snelled hooks because bait can be slipped right over the leader knot. Too, a properly snelled hook will give a direct pull from leader to hook, often essential to consistently hook fish.

Fig. 1 Thread the leader through the hook eye, and lay the leader along the hook shank.

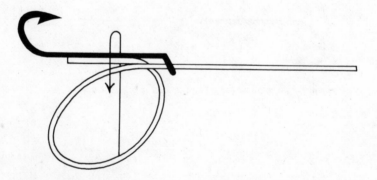

Fig. 2 Pull about six inches of leader through the hook eye, and form a loop below the hook shank, as shown.

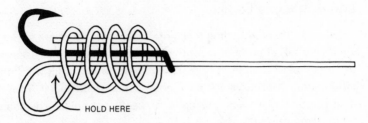

Fig. 3 Hold the two lines parallel to the hook against the hook shank. Then wrap the loop over the entire hook so that the line of the loop that's closest to the hook eye forms a series of coils.

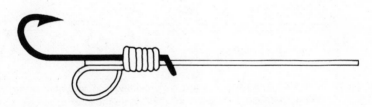

Fig. 4 After six tight coils are formed on the hook shank, slowly pull on the standing part of the line. This will bring the loop through the coils and tighten the knot.

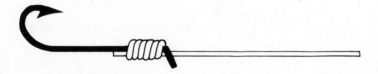

Fig. 5 The completed Snell.

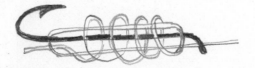

BOB MCNALLY'S LOOP

Although there are some types of "loop knots" that are stronger, such as the Nail Loop, this loop is one of the fastest and easiest to tie. It is most valuable to anglers who want a knot that will form a loop so that their lures will have good action in the water. Too, this loop can be tied in seconds, making it useful to anglers who change lures frequently.

The Bob McNally Loop is used often by ice fishermen to tie on ice fishing jigs. The loop can be tied easily when wearing gloves, and it allows an ice lure to "wiggle" freely when "jigged" by the angler.

Fig. 1 Put the leader through the lure's connecting ring, and double the line, leaving about eight inches with which to tie the knot.

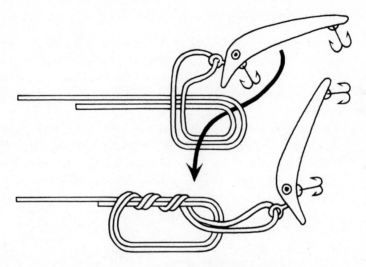

Figs. 2 & 3 Pinch the end of the line against the standing part of the line. Now form a loop with the doubled line and make three Overhand Knots with the lure.

Fig. 4 Pull the lure and the standing part of the line to tighten the knot.

DOUBLE WEMYSS KNOT

The Double Wemyss Knot is not as good as some knots designed for turned-down hook eyes, such as the Double Turle Knot. However, this knot is fast to tie and untie, and is an adequate connection when a situation arises requiring that a knot be tied as speedily as possible.

The Double Wemyss Knot is easy to make. First, thread the line through the hook eye. Take the end of the line and loop it once around the standing line. Then double the end of the line back and wrap it twice around the standing line near the hook eye. Now take the first loop, slide it over the hook eye, and slowly tighten the knot so that the finished knot is behind the "eye."

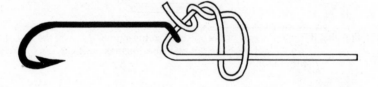

IMPROVED CLINCH KNOT (Also known as Pandre Knot or Jam Knot With An Extra Tuck)

The Improved Clinch Knot is one of the most popular knots for tying a line or a leader to either a hook or a lure eye. It is one of the most dependable and secure knots.

Although many anglers still insist on using the ordinary Clinch Knot, the Improved Clinch Knot is just as easy to tie and it is about 20 percent stronger.

This knot can be difficult to tighten when using heavy-test monofilament, but if the tie is moistened well the knot usually will tighten properly.

Fig. 1 Pass the end of the line through the hook eye. Put about six inches of line through the eye so there will be ample line with which to tie the knot.

Fig. 2 Hold the hook or lure securely in one hand and wrap the end of the line five times around the standing part of the line, as shown in the illustration. Now pass the end of the line back through the small loop near the hook eye, and also through the large loop.

Fig. 3 Tighten and trim the knot carefully.

NAIL LOOP KNOT

This is by far the best and most reliable knot for tying a loop to a fly or lure so that it can "swim" and "wiggle" freely for the best action.

Although the Nail Loop is more difficult to tie than some loop knots, such as the Homer Rhode Loop and Dave Hawk's Drop Loop Knot, it is much stronger and is recommended over those knots.

Fig. 1 Put the line end through the hook eye, leaving about eight inches with which to tie the knot. Lay the line end parallel to the standing part and place a nail, tube, or toothpick between the two strands. Then make three and one-half wraps with the end of the line back towards the hook eye.

Fig. 2 Next slip the line end forward through the loops made by turning the line over the two parallel strands.

Fig. 3 When this knot is tied carefully and the loops are pulled tight, the knot should look like this.

TAUTLINE HITCH KNOT

This is a sliding loop knot that is quite easy to tie and a valuable one to any angler. When a Tautline Hitch is employed a loop of any size may be formed, so that a lure will "wiggle" freely when retrieved. When a fish is hooked, the knot slides down and "jams" against the hook eye. After the fish is landed the knot can be opened again to re-form its loop.

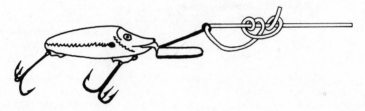

Fig. 1 Pass the end of the line through the hook eye. Bring the line end forward and wrap it around the standing part of the line twice. Next bring the end in front of the first wrap and wind it around the standing part of the line.

Fig. 2 The finished Tautline Hitch.

SLIDING OVERHEAD KNOT

It takes practice to tie this knot quickly, but the practice is worth it since this is a good, strong knot, especially useful in knotting braided line.

The trick in tying this knot is to be sure *both loops* slip back over the hook eye before pulling the knot tight.

LARK'S HEAD KNOT

The Lark's Head Knot is used extensively by natural bait fishermen for tying on hooks, and by some other anglers for attaching swivels and lures to line or leader. It can be tied and untied quickly, which is advantageous at times when it is necessary to change lures fast.

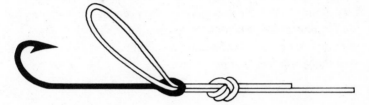

Fig. 1 A loop is formed at the end of the line or leader, and then the loop is passed through the hook, lure, or swivel "eye."

Fig. 2 The loop is passed over the lure or swivel.

Fig. 3 The knot is then pulled tight.

JANSIK SPECIAL KNOT

Few anglers are familiar with the Jansik Special, unfortunately, because it is a superb knot to tie with monofilament line.

This knot is not difficult to tie, and with a little practice it can be done in a few seconds.

To tie the Jansik Special, pass the end of the line through the hook eye twice. Then bring the line back around again, as though you were going to put the line through the hook eye three times. Wrap the tag end of the line three times around the monofilament loops. Pull the knot smoothly and carefully until tight. Moistening the knot with saliva will help tighten it.

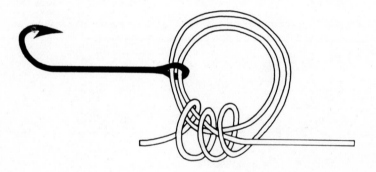

CLINCH KNOT (Also referred to as Half-Blood Knot and Stevedore Knot)

The Clinch Knot is probably the favorite knot among skilled anglers for tying a line to a hook or lure eye. It is a very secure, fast tie, and it can be made with heavy monofilament, too. When tying the Clinch Knot with heavy mono it's best to make only three or four turns rather than the standard five turns. This way the knot will tighten easier, yet will not lose much of its strength.

Fig. 1 Pass the end of the leader or line through the hook eye, and pull about six inches of line through to tie the knot. Bring the end of the line back toward the standing part and wrap the end five times around the standing line. Next pass the line end back through the first loop.

Fig. 2 Slowly pull on the standing part of the line, and the line's end, until the turns in the knot draw tightly against the hook eye.

DAVE HAWK'S DROP-LOOP KNOT

Although this knot takes time to tie, even by an expert, it is a superb, firm connection. The Drop-Loop Knot is good because it allows a lure or fly to vibrate and wiggle freely, since the knot forms a loop rather than a tight tie against the lure.

Many plastic worm fishermen use this knot, as well as fishermen using deep-running, wobbling plugs.

This is also an excellent knot to use with very heavy monofilament line.

Fig. 1 Tie a regular Overhand Knot in the line about five inches from its end and pull tight.

Fig. 2 Pass the end of the line through the lure's connecting ring and bring it back parallel to the standing part of the line. Turn the line end down, forming a circle below the two parallel strands. Turn the line end around both parallel lines and through the circle twice, as shown.

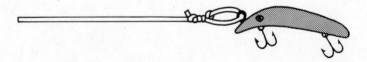

Fig. 3 Slowly draw the knot tight. Pull on the line and lure simultaneously so that the knot will slide down and pull up tight against the Overhand Knot.

PRIMA KNOT

This knot originated in Germany for tying nylon to hook eyes. However, it is extremely difficult to tie even for an expert with good eyesight. That probably is why so few anglers use the Prima Knot.

Thread the leader through the hook eye, leaving at least six inches of leader with which to tie the knot. Next, form a loop with the end of the line and make a Double Overhand Knot, letting it hang below the hook. Then make a loop in the standing part of the leader, pass the loop through the opening of the Double Overhand Knot, and then loop it over the hook.

Slowly pull the Double Overhand Knot tight with the tag end of the leader, then pull the standing part of the line to tighten the knot behind the hook eye.

When this knot is tied properly it will form a secure connection, with the leader coming straight up and out from under the hook eye. The finished Prima Knot should look much like a completed Turle Knot.

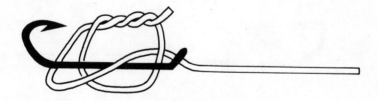

RETURN JAM KNOT

This knot is merely another variation of the Return Knot. It can be difficult to tie, but with practice an angler can make this knot in seconds.

The Return Jam Knot is easier to tie with light monofilament than with braided line or heavy test nylon.

The knot was designed for tying nylon to turned-up or turned-down hook eyes, and it is a strong and dependable knot when properly tied.

Fig. 1 Pass the leader through the hook eye and loosely wrap the line end around the hook shank.

Fig. 2 Bring the line end around the standing part of the line.

Fig. 3 Put the line end through the first loop made around the hook shank.

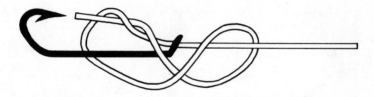

Fig. 4 Make an Overhand Knot around the standing line behind the hook eye.

Fig. 5 The finished Return Jam Knot.

DOUBLE EYE KNOT

The Double Eye Knot is a quick, secure tie that is often employed by fishermen using natural bait.

It is a satisfactory knot for use with all types of hooks, however, it is especially good on hooks having turned-up or turned-down "eyes."

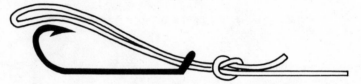

Fig. 1 Double the line, forming a loop, then tie a simple Overhand Knot over the standing line. Pass the loop through the hook eye.

Fig. 2 The loop now goes over the bend of the hook, and is pulled up to the hook eye.

Fig. 3 Take the "tag end" of the Overhand Knot and pass it under the loop, against the hook shank, and draw the knot tight.

Fig. 4 The completed Double Eye Knot.

Regardless of what kind of fishing is being done, special care must be taken in tying all knots. This sea trout hit a fly fisherman's streamer.

FIGURE EIGHT KNOT

A fast knot to tie, the Figure Eight for that reason frequently is selected by anglers who want to change lures or flies quickly. There are many fishing situations in which a nearly instant change of lures is vitally important. This is particularly true in fly fishing, where, for example, a fish that refuses one fly may be caught if the angler swiftly presents a different pattern to the fish.

The Figure Eight Knot holds best when tied with wire or braided line, not so well when tied with monofilament.

To tie a Figure Eight, put the end of the line through the hook eye, bring it back over the standing part of the line, and pass the line end back through the loop near the hook eye. Hold the hook or lure securely and pull the knot tight.

QUICK SNELL KNOT

This is a good knot for snelling a hook quickly. The Quick Snell Knot isn't as neat nor does it hold as well as a regular snell; however, the Quick Snell is much easier to tie.

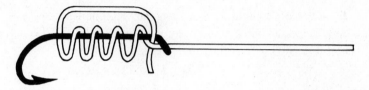

Fig. 1 The hook eye is threaded with the line end. Then the line is wrapped four times around the hook shank. Next the line is put through the loop that's between the first wrap and the hook eye.

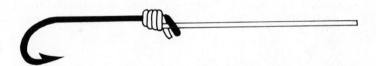

Fig. 2 The tag end and the standing part of the line are tightened until the knot appears as illustrated.

TWO CIRCLE TURLE KNOT

This is one of the most-used knots in Europe for tying a hook or fly to a nylon leader. As with all variations of the Turle Knot, the Two Circle Turle Knot is normally used to tie flies with a turned-up or turned-down eye to a leader.

Most fishermen believe that the Turle Knot was invented by a Major Turle of England. However, as the Major himself reported, he didn't design the many different Turle Knots but rather learned them from his numerous fishing companions.

Fig. 1 Push the leader end through the hook eye, and slide the hook up the leader out of the way. Form a circle with the leader about six inches from the leader's end.

Fig. 2 Make a second loop identical to the first, and overlay the two loops.

Fig. 3 Now tie an Overhand Knot over the two loops, as illustrated, and tighten it.

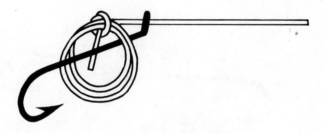

Fig. 4 Put the hook, lure, or fly through the two loops.

Fig. 5 Pull on the leader end and its standing part until the knot tightens behind the hook eye. The trimmed, finished knot is shown.

DOUBLE-LOOP IMPROVED CLINCH KNOT

This is a Double-Loop Clinch Knot carried one step further. The line end is passed through the hook eye twice. The line is wrapped four times around its standing part, then it is passed through the two loops near the "eye." The final step is to put the line end through the large loop, as shown.

The Double-Loop Improved Clinch Knot isn't difficult to tie. It's a very strong connection. Moreover, one very large fishing tackle company even recommends the use of this knot with all of its lures.

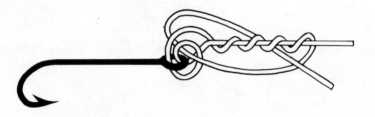

DOUBLE SHEET BEND KNOT

The Double Sheet Bend Knot is much more versatile and stronger than the Single Sheet Bend.

The Double Sheet Bend can be knotted fast, yet it makes an adequate connection for specific angling situations, such as fishing for panfish.

Too, the Double Sheet Bend is a valuable knot to most fishermen because it can be used to quickly form a "loop," which gives a lure or fly better action, or it can be drawn tight against the hook eye.

Fig. 1 Put the line through the hook eye. Wrap the line end around the standing part of the line, and make an Overhand Knot. This will form a "slip knot."

Fig. 2 Pull the knot tight. If desired the Double Sheet Bend can be tightened above the hook eye to form a loop, or "jammed" tight against the hook eye as shown.

TWO-WRAP HANGMAN'S KNOT (Also called Figure Eight Knot)

This is a very valuable knot for any angler. The knot forms a loop so that a lure or fly will have more action in the water. It can be tied with either heavy or light monofilament.

The Two-Wrap Hangman's Knot is a sliding loop knot, so it can be tightened anywhere on the standing part of the fishing line, and a loop of any size can be made. In addition, when a fish strikes and is hooked, the knot will slide down and tighten against the hook eye. After the fish is landed, the knot can be slipped open and another loop formed.

Fig. 1 Thread the line end through the hook eye, and then make two wraps around the standing line back toward the hook eye. Keep the loops loose, holding them open with your fingers.

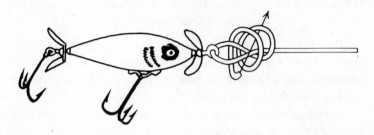

Fig. 2 Push the line end back through the two loops, away from the hook or lure.

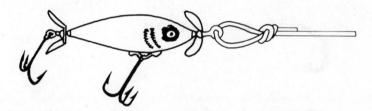

Fig. 3 Stick the hook or lure into a piece of wood or anything else solid. Then pull slowly on the standing part and tag ends of the knot. When the knot is almost tight, it can be slid up or down the leader, forming whatever size loop is desired, before the knot is pulled completely tight.

CADENAS KNOT (Sometimes referred to as Double Hitch Jam Knot or Double Overhand Jam Knot)

This knot is used by many anglers in Europe, and, in fact, it was originated in France. The Cadenas Knot was designed for tying Japanese silkworm "gut" leaders to a hook eye. However, it is a fine knot to use with nylon monofilament and braided line.

Some anglers use this knot instead of a Turle Knot because the Cadenas Knot makes a straight-line connection from hook eye to leader, and it is particularly effective when used with hooks that have turned-up or turned-down eyes.

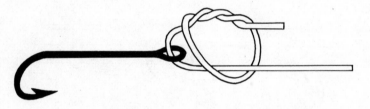

Fig. 1 Put the line end through the hook eye. Then bring the line back around the standing part of the line, forming a circle. Now wind the line end twice around the top of the loop that was formed, as in making a Double Overhand Knot.

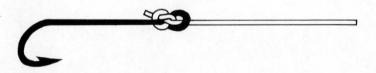

Fig. 2 Slide the loop back over the hook eye, and slowly pull the knot snug.

FAST SWIVEL KNOT

When tied properly the Fast Swivel Knot is a satisfactory connection for many fishing situations. It is popular with anglers who use barrel swivels. Many fishermen who do a lot of motor trolling use this knot, and so do some plastic worm fishermen who use barrel swivels to prevent line twist.

Although this knot is primarily used with swivels, it also can be tied to a lure or hook. However, it isn't as secure as some other knots, such as the Improved Clinch Knot.

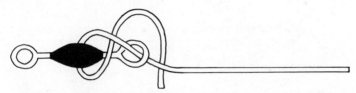

Fig. 1 Thread the swivel eye with the line end. Wrap the line end around the swivel once, then under the standing part of the line and back over the swivel again.

Fig. 2 The line end comes completely under the standing part of the line in front of the swivel, and then through the two loops, as illustrated.

Fig. 3 Both loops of the knot are tightened behind the swivel eye, and the knot is finished.

CLINCH ON SHANK KNOT

Although the Clinch On Shank Knot is difficult to tie, it is popular among bait fishermen. Bait fishermen like this knot because it is strong and it permits a very direct pull right from the center of the hook eye.

The most important aspect of tying this knot is to *slowly* pull and form the tie before tightening and trimming.

Leaping pavon, hooked in Brazil's Araquaia River, tests quality of fisherman's knots.

DOUBLE SNELLING KNOTS (Commonly called Double Salmon Knots)

Many coho and Chinook salmon anglers in the Great Lakes area and on the West Coast use two, three, four—sometimes even six—snelled hooks at the same time, each threaded with a natural bait. This is the best knot to use when snelling more than one hook on a leader.

The Double Snelled Knot takes time and is difficult to tie, but it is an extremely durable connection.

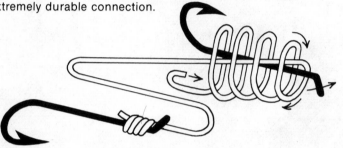

Fig. 1 Snell the lower hook first. Then take the leader from the hook already snelled and loosely wind the end of the leader over the standing part of the leader and the shank of the second hook. Push the leader end through the loose loops.

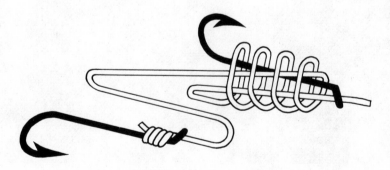

Fig. 2 The leader end must be passed through all of the loops to make the knot secure. Then the tag end and the standing part of the leader are slowly tightened.

EYE-CROSSER KNOT

Very few anglers use the Eye-Crosser Knot because it was developed only recently. This knot is excellent with braided and nylon monofilament lines, and can be easily tied with almost any test line.

The Eye-Crosser Knot is popular with southern bass fishermen who need a knot that is strong and won't pull out when heavy bass are hooked in brushy, snag-filled areas.

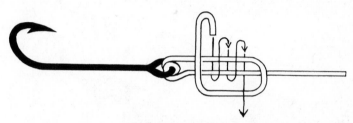

Fig. 1 Pass the line end through the hook eye twice, leaving about eight inches with which to tie the knot. Bring the line end back parallel to the standing line, and pinch the two lines together with the thumb and forefinger about two inches in front of the hook eye.

Fig. 2 Wrap the line end around the two parallel strands three times, and pass the line end through the loop.

Fig. 3 Finally, pull on the standing part of the line to bring the knot tight against the hook eye.

TURLE KNOT

This is an old and reliable knot that's particularly popular with fly fishermen. The Turle Knot is quick and simple to tie. Also, it is extremely valuable to anglers because it is designed specifically for tying on hooks that have turned-down or turned-up eyes.

Because the leader (or line) passes through the hook eye, in line with the shank, when you strike fish the hook moves in a direct line. That helps considerably in sinking the barb.

(For more information on this knot, turn to page 148.)

Fig. 1 The line end goes through the hook eye, and a loop is formed in the line. A simple Overhand Knot is tied around the standing part of the line.

Fig. 2 The loop is enlarged enough so that the fly passes through.

Fig. 3 With the loop tight behind the hook eye, the knot is pulled tight against the neck of the fly.

Fig. 4 The leader is drawn tight through the hook eye, and the line end is trimmed close to the knot.

RETURN KNOT

This knot was designed for tying monofilament leaders to a fly, lure, or hook eye. Although comparatively few anglers are familiar with the Return Knot, it is very strong and not difficult to tie. This is a particularly valuable knot for tying heavy test nylon to flies or lures.

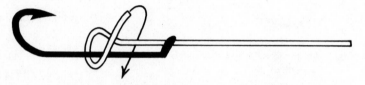

Fig. 1 Put the end of the line through the hook eye. Wrap the line around the hook, and hold the loop between your thumb and forefinger.

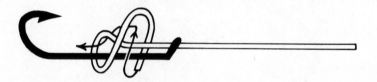

Fig. 2 Make a second turn, like the first, and again hold the loop.

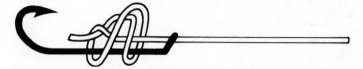

Fig. 3 Pass the end of the line under both loops, and slowly pull on the standing part of the line. As the knot tightens be sure both loops are on the shank side of the hook eye.

Fig. 4 The completed knot, tightened and trimmed.

OFFSHORE SWIVEL KNOT

The Offshore Swivel Knot is a strong, reliable knot that can be used not only for securing heavy-duty swivels to a fishing line, but also for tying monofilament line to a hook eye or to a lure's connecting ring.

The Swivel Knot is easier to tie than it looks, and moistening the wraps with saliva helps to tighten it.

If one strand of the doubled line breaks, the Swivel Knot will still hold securely with the remaining strand.

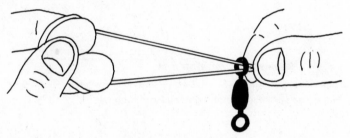

Fig. 1 Make a doubled line—using a good knot such as the Bimini Twist or Spider Hitch—at the end of the fishing line. Insert the doubled line through one "eye" of a heavy-duty swivel.

Fig. 2 Bring the end of the doubled line back, and pinch it to the standing part of the doubled line.

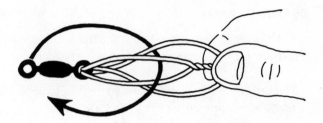

Fig. 3 Pass the swivel through both loops of the doubled line.

Fig. 4 Pass the swivel through both loops six or seven times, and the knot will look like this.

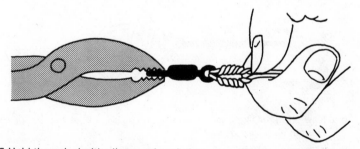

Fig. 5 Hold the swivel with pliers, and push the wraps of the knot tight against the swivel to tighten the knot.

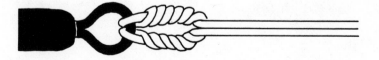

Fig. 6 The completed Offshore Swivel Knot.

CRAWFORD KNOT

The Crawford Knot often is overlooked by even the most skilled anglers. It is a very versatile knot for tying most types of hook, swivel, or lure "eyes" to a leader or line.

The Crawford Knot is not nearly so difficult to tie as it looks, and it makes a solid, firm connection.

Fig. 1 Insert the line through the hook eye, leaving about eight inches for tying the knot. Bring the line end back around the standing part of the line to form a loop.

Fig. 2 Now bring the line end under the standing part of the line, and *over* the two parallel lines, as shown.

Fig. 3 The knot has formed a "figure 8." Bring the tag end of the line under the two parallel strands, then back over all three lines.

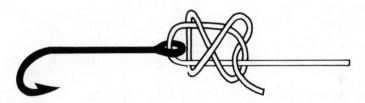

Fig. 4 The knot is completed by tucking the tag end between the standing line and the front part of the loop. Pull the knot tight, slide it down and "jam" it against the hook eye and trim.

4 Loops and Specialty Knots

There are many line connections and arrangements employed by fishermen to fulfill special fishing needs. An example is the line rigging called "Making A Loop To Carry A Large Fish," which is one of the "specialty" knots in this chapter.

However, most of this chapter is dedicated to the forming and tying of various kinds of loops. Loops are essential, in one form or another, in almost all types of fishing, in all areas.

One of the most famous and valued "loops," or specialty knots, included in this chapter is the Bimini Twist. The Bimini Twist is used to form a doubled line, and is of vital importance when severe line end wear is likely.

END LOOP KNOT

This loop knot is much easier to tie than it appears. With very little practice it can be tied in just a few seconds.

The End Loop works equally well with braided lines or monofilament. And, too, this knot is often used by some anglers who want a double line that is stronger than the standing part of the single line.

Fig. 1 Double the end of the line, leaving about six inches of doubled line with which to tie the knot.

Fig. 2 Wind the doubled line back over itself five times.

Fig. 3 Take the end of the doubled line and pass it through the first loop. Now tighten the knot by pulling on the standing line and the tag end, as well as on the doubled line.

Fig. 4 The finished End Loop.

KNOT FOR FASTENING LINE TO REEL

This is the quickest and easiest way of tying monofilament or braided line to any type reel.

First pass the line around the reel spool, and tie a simple Overhand Knot in the line. Now tie another Overhand Knot with the short end of the line around the standing part of the line. Pull the second knot tight, and tug on the standing part of the line to bring both of the Overhand Knots together. Trim the short end of the knot, then reel the line onto the reel.

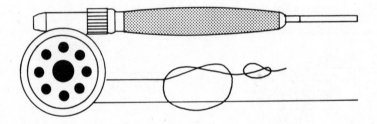

MAKING A LOOP TO CARRY A LARGE FISH

Although this is quite an elaborate way to make a loop to carry a fish, it actually is very useful to anglers who must walk long distances to and from their fishing area.

This loop is used often by salmon anglers, particularly in the Great Lakes area, who fish the feeder rivers where large coho and Chinook salmon run up each fall. When a large fish is caught, this frequently is the most practical way to carry it.

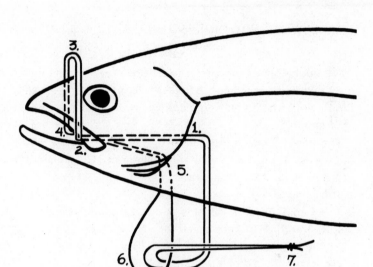

Fig. 1 Double a piece of heavy line so that it's about five feet long, and tie the two ends together.

1. Push one end of the doubled line under the fish's gill plate . . .
2. . . . and out the near corner of its mouth.
3. Then pull the end of the doubled line over the fish's nose.
4. Now push the same line end into the far corner of its mouth . . .
5. . . . and out under the fish's gill plate.
6. Pull the loop down under the fish . . .
7. . . . and insert the other end of the doubled line through the loop.

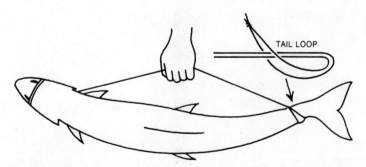

Fig. 2 Form a loop at the opposite end of the doubled line, and slip the loop over the fish's tail, as shown.

BIMINI TWIST KNOT (Often referred to as 20 Times Around Knot,
Rollover Knot, and The 100 Percent Knot)

Although some knots perform equally as well as the Bimini, and
are easier to tie (such as the Spider Hitch), many anglers still prefer
the Bimini Twist for making a double line that will have 100 percent
knot strength.

The Bimini Twist is often used by salt water anglers who want a
double line for use with offshore trolling rigs. Too, some fishermen
use this knot for making a "shock tippet" to use with fly or
bait-casting tackle.

The Bimini Twist is valuable because it doubles the test of the
single strand of line with which the knot is made.

Although this knot can be tied by one person, it's much easier to
make it with the aid of an assistant.

Fig. 1 Double the end of the line along the standing part of the line, for about
four feet. Then twist the line 20 times, creating loops, as shown.

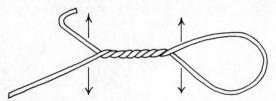

Fig. 2 Pull all four ends apart so that the 20 twists will be forced tightly
together, leaving a wide loop.

Fig. 3 Keep the twists tightly together, and begin winding the end of the line
back over the twists.

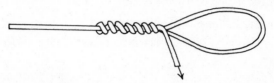

Fig. 4 Continue winding the end of the line over the twists until the line reaches the loop.

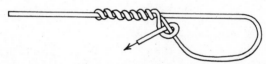

Fig. 5 Hold the end of the twists with one hand, and make an Overhand Knot around one side of the loop.

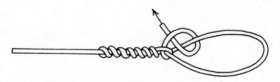

Fig. 6 Make an Overhand Knot around the other side of the loop. (Some anglers make this Overhand Knot around the two lines of the loop rather than around just one side and then the other.)

Fig. 7 Wind the line end three times around the two lines of the large loop, and push the end back through the small loop just made.

Fig. 8 Slowly pull on the standing line and the large loop to draw the Bimini Twist tight.

FORMING A FLY LINE LOOP (II)

Some fly rodders shy away from fly line loops because they're too bulky. However, when made properly, this type of fly line loop is extremely strong.

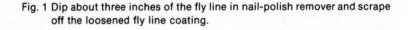

Fig. 1 Dip about three inches of the fly line in nail-polish remover and scrape off the loosened fly line coating.

Fig. 2 Fold the scraped fly line back, forming a loop.

Fig. 3 Wrap the two scraped fly lines tightly together with size 00 nylon thread. Then lacquer or varnish the tie.

LEADER LOOP KNOT

The Leader Loop Knot is a good, strong knot for tying a loop in a line to which a leader may be attached. It can be tied quickly.

This loop is best when used with stiff monofilament or a fly line, rather than with braided lines. The Leader Loop Knot works well with braided lines, but is difficult to tie with them because of their limpness.

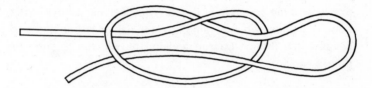

Fig. 1 Tie a loose Overhand Knot about six inches from the end of the line. Pass the end of the line through the center of the Overhand Knot.

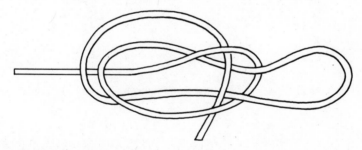

Fig. 2 The end of the line is then brought around the Overhand Knot and passed through the two openings of the knot.

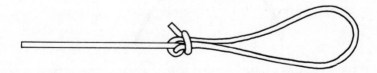

Fig. 3 The finished Leader Loop Knot after the tag end has been trimmed.

MAKING A PERMANENT LOOP IN DACRON LINE

This loop can be made in Dacron line very quickly. It is extremely strong and is valuable because it eliminates the need for a bulky knot. This loop won't pull out because the line end is pushed through the standing part of the line for at least eight inches.

Because a knot isn't used to make this tie, it goes through rod guides very smoothly. For that reason, some fly fishermen prefer to make a "Permanent Loop" in Dacron "backing" line and connect it to a loop at the end of their fly line. They feel that the connection is a good one to use when angling for such fish as tarpon and bonefish, because the fly line-Dacron backing tie will run through the rod guides easily.

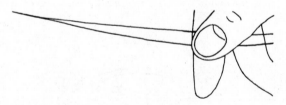

Fig. 1 Bend a piece of light, thin wire into a sharp "V."

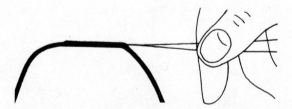

Fig. 2 Insert the pointed end of the wire "V" into the center of the Dacron line. Where you insert the wire will determine the size of the loop to be formed.

Fig. 3 Push the wire through and out of the Dacron line, about eight inches from where the wire was inserted.

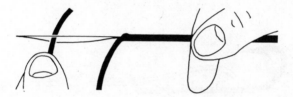

Fig. 4 Secure the end of the Dacron line in the wire loop.

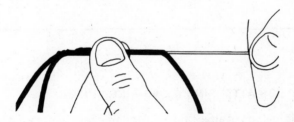

Fig. 5 Withdraw the wire "V" from the Dacron, which in turn will pull the end of the Dacron line through the center of the standing part of the line.

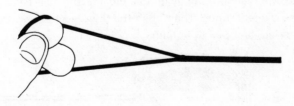

Fig. 6 The completed loop.

SPLIT-SHOT SINKER LOOP

This loop eliminates tying and untying knots to a lure or hook. The line is doubled, and a split-shot sinker is clamped around the two lines to form a loop. The loop is then slipped over the lure or hook, as shown, which secures the tie.

This loop is not recommended when angling for large fish. But it is an adequate tie for panfish, and is used often by some southern anglers.

SPLIT-SHOT
SINKER

LOOP FOR ATTACHING A TWO-RING SINKER

This method of attaching a two-ring sinker often is used by anglers fishing natural baits for panfish. It is beneficial to those anglers because the sinker can be put on or removed in seconds, or easily adjusted anywhere on the fishing line.

To form the loop, simply double the line and insert it through both of the sinker's rings. Then push the line end through the loop, as illustrated, and pull to tighten.

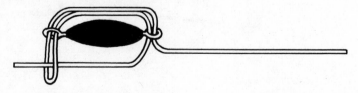

DOUBLE LINE LOOP KNOT

The Double Line Loop is difficult to tie. It can be used to make a permanent loop in the end of a line, to which leaders may be tied. Too, this knot may be used to create a "double line" that's stronger than the single line.

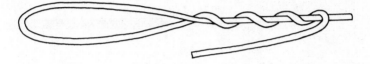

Fig. 1 Double the line and wind the end of the line four times over the standing part, leaving a large loop.

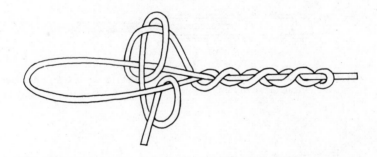

Fig. 2 Wind the line end four times back over the wraps just made. Then, with the end of the line, make a simple Overhand Knot around one side of the loop, and tie a Half-Hitch around the other side of the loop.

FORMING A FLY LINE LOOP (I)

Many fly anglers prefer Forming A Fly Line Loop and tying their leader butts to it, rather than using a Nail Knot for the connection.

Although A Fly Line Loop, when properly formed, is very strong, the loop won't go through a rod's guides as easily as a Nail Knot.

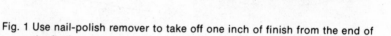

Fig. 1 Use nail-polish remover to take off one inch of finish from the end of the fly line.

Fig. 2 Take a three-inch piece of bait-casting line (15–20 lb. test), and double it over the cleaned fly line.

Fig. 3 Tightly wrap over the two ends of bait-casting line and fly line with size 00 nylon thread. Varnish or lacquer the joint.

SINGLE OVERHAND LOOP KNOT (Occasionally called Overhand Eye Knot and Common Loop Knot)

This is the easiest knot for making a loop in the end of a length of line. Simply double the line, and make an Overhand Knot.

This is not the strongest knot to use in making a line loop. However, for most light, fresh water angling it is an adequate tie.

Tarpon fishermen use the Bimini Twist Knot to form a doubled line, often needed in handling tough-fighting "silver kings."

IMPROVED DROPPER LOOP (Also known as Blood Dropper Loop)

The Improved Dropper Loop is very popular with fly anglers who fish more than one fly simultaneously. The loop can be tied quickly and it is secure. Once the loop is tied, another leader with a fly attached may be tied to the loop.

In recent years some inventive fishermen have begun using this loop with bait casting and spinning equipment. A deep-running lure is tied to the fishing line's end in the conventional manner, then one or two Improved Dropper Loops are tied above the first lure. Other leaders with lures attached are then tied to the loops, and such a rig can make an unusual and often productive trolling outfit.

Fig. 1 A two- or three-inch loop is formed in the line. The two lines that cross to form the loop are pinched, and the loop is twisted five times around the two crossed lines. When this is done correctly the loop should appear as in the illustration.

Fig. 2 The center of the twisted lines is opened and the loop is pushed through.

Fig. 3 Now the two ends of the line are drawn slowly tight. A finger or pencil placed in the loop will prevent the loop from pulling out.

Fig. 4 The finished Improved Dropper Loop.

PERFECTION LOOP KNOT (Commonly called Perfection Leader End Loop, Fishermen's Loop, and Compound Knot)

This is one of the best knots known for tying a loop in the end of a line, particularly nylon monofilament line.

Although the Perfection Loop Knot is difficult to tie the first few times, after a while it becomes quite easy. The trick to tying this knot is to simultaneously pull the loop, the standing part of the leader, and the tag end of the leader until the knot is tight.

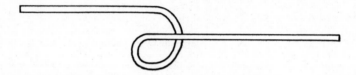

Fig. 1 Form a loop about six inches from the end of the line.

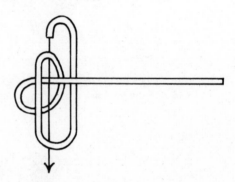

Fig. 2 Now, with the end of the line, make a loop over the first loop. Then pass the end of the line under the loop just made, as shown.

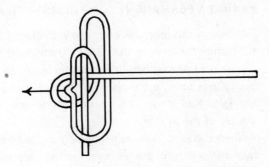

Fig. 3 Pull the end of the second loop through the opening of the first loop.

Fig. 4 Tighten the knot by pulling firmly on the second loop while also holding the standing line taut.

MAKING A PERMANENT LOOP IN MONOFILAMENT FLY LINE

Although this loop can be made with any type of fly line, it is used most often for looping the new monofilament fly lines.

To make this loop, double back the fly line to form the desired size loop. Then, using a couple of lenghts of light monofilament line, tie two Fast Nail Knots, about one-fourth inch apart, around both strands of the fly line.

When this loop is made properly it is remarkably strong, and it will pass through rod guides easily when connected to a fly fishing leader or to a backing line.

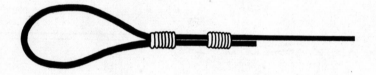

BOWLINE (Also known as Bowling)

Although the Bowline is normally considered a boating knot, it is also a very valuable knot to anglers.

A Bowline can be used to put a loop in the end of a line so that a leader may be attached. Too, the Bowline is excellent for tying a "loop knot" onto a lure so that the lure "swims" more freely when it's retrieved.

The Bowline can be tied in seconds. It will not slip and is extremely strong.

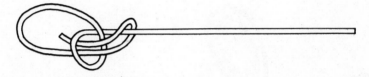

Fig. 1 Form a loop in the line about four inches from the line's end. Push the end of the line through the loop, around the standing part of the line, and out the loop again.

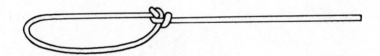

Fig. 2 Pull on the tag end and the standing part of the line to tighten the knot.

SPIDER HITCH KNOT

Many anglers around the country are now using the Spider Hitch instead of the Bimini Twist when they want a knot that will double their line. The Spider Hitch can be quickly tied; it has superb knot strength; and it can be tied easily by one person (the Bimini Twist is best tied by two people.)

The Spider Hitch can be tied effortlessly—with either nylon monofilament or braided lines—to form a double line having twice the strength of a single strand.

Fig. 1 Double the line, then put a small reverse loop in it.

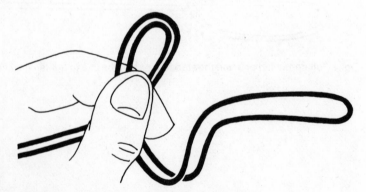

Fig. 2 Hold the reverse loop with thumb and forefinger.

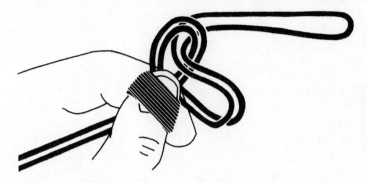

Fig. 3 Wrap the doubled line five times around the thumb and the reverse loop. Then pass the large loop through the small reverse loop.

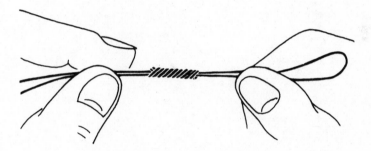

Fig. 4 Slowly pull the large loop so that the line unwinds off the thumb, pulling until the knot tightens.

DOUBLE OVERHAND KNOT (Also called Two Fold Water Knot, Two Fold Blood Knot, Line Knot, and Surgeon's Double Loop)

This is an easily tied and reliable knot for putting a loop in the end of a line or leader.

To tie this knot simply double the line, and make two Overhand Knots with the doubled line.

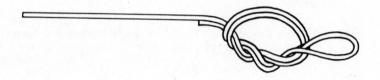

LOOP FOR ATTACHING A SINGLE "EYE" SINKER

Many fishermen who use natural baits tie a dropper line a foot or so above the baited hook, and then tie a single-eye sinker to it. This loop is an excellent way of attaching a single-eye sinker to a dropper line because the sinker may be put on or removed easily.

Getting a sinker on or off the line quickly is helpful when changing sinkers frequently in the course of a day's fishing.

Fig. 1 Tie a loop in the end of the leader or line.

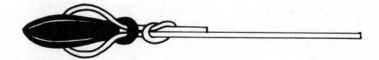

Fig. 2 Pass the loop through the "eye" of the sinker, then slip the loop over the sinker.

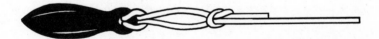

Fig. 3 Pull on the standing part of the line to draw the knot tight against the sinker's "eye."

JAPANESE FISHERMAN'S KNOT

Although this knot looks similar to the Double Line Loop and Bimini Twist, it is in fact a different knot. However, it is used for the same purposes as those two knots.

Many anglers feel that the Japanese Fisherman's Knot is the easiest knot to tie in making a double line. They believe that the Double Line Loop and Bimini Twist take too long to tie, and certainly they require much more "finger dexterity" than the average angler possesses.

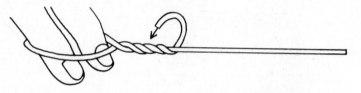

Fig. 1 Double the line, then wind the end of the line five times over the standing part, holding the loop open with the fingers.

Fig. 2 Wrap the end of the line five times back over the wraps just made.

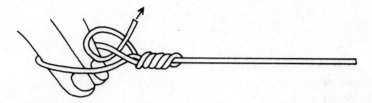

Fig. 3 Take the end of the line, pass it through the loop, and tie a Half-Hitch.

Fig. 4 Pass the end of the line forward and under the "wraps," tie another Half-Hitch through the loop, then tighten.

5 Knots For Fly Fishing

Some of the knots in this chapter appear elsewhere in the book. However, they are knots of special use to fly fishermen, and therefore are presented in this chapter. By having all knots of any practical use to fly fishermen grouped together in a single, separate chapter, a fly angler can immediately locate, and learn to tie, the knots that fill his specific needs.

The knots in the followinging grouping are considered the best possible ties for fly fishing.

JOINING TWO LOOPS

Many fly fishermen join monofilament leaders to their fly lines, and backing lines to their fly lines, with this loop connection.

A Nail Knot can be made much more quickly and is less bulky, but this connection is adequate for many types of fly angling—provided the two loops are properly made and joined.

(For more information on this knot, turn to page 41.)

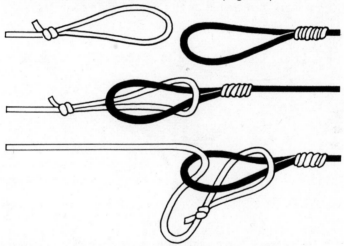

Fig. 1 Pass one loop through the opening of the other loop. Then pull the line of the second loop through the first loop, as shown.

Fig. 2 When the two loops are drawn tight they should look like this.

TURLE KNOT

There are stronger knots to use for fastening a leader to a fly, but the Turle Knot is useful when tying on hooks having turned-up or turned-down "eyes."

When a Turle Knot is tied properly, the leader will come away from a turned hook eye in a straight line. This helps when fishing dry flies because the fly will "ride" the surface better.

(For more information on this knot, turn to page 112.)

Fig. 1 The line end goes through the hook eye, a simple Overhand Knot is tied around the standing part of the line, and a loop is formed in the line.

Fig. 2 Pass the fly through the loop.

Fig. 3 With the loop snug behind the hook eye, the knot is pulled tight against the fly's neck.

Fig. 4 The leader is drawn through the hook eye, and the line end trimmed close to the knot.

A Bivisible dry fly skimmed over the surface fooled this stocky rainbow trout.
A Portland Creek Hitch (Riffling Hitch) Knot, helped keep the fly riding high
during the retrieve.

EXTENSION BLOOD KNOT

This is the strongest and most popular way to attach "dropper lines" for fishing two or more flies simultaneously.

Often the Extension Blood Knot is not as convenient to tie as some other dropper knots. For example, if the fly fishing leader is already "made up," it must be cut and rejoined if an Extension Blood Knot is to be employed. But when an angler knows while making up his leader that he wants to use a dropper fly or two—this is *always* the knot that should be used.

(For more information on this knot, turn to page 23.)

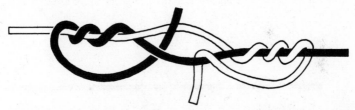

Fig. 1 Wind one leader strand three times around the standing part of the second leader strand, and bring the end back behind the first turn. Do the same with the other leader end, and the knot should appear as in the drawing.

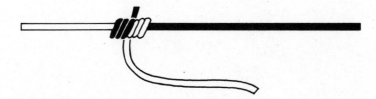

Fig. 2 Pull on the standing part of both leader strands to draw the knot tight. Trim *only one* of the tag ends of the knot. The other tag end becomes the dropper line for attaching a fly.

PENDRE DROPPER KNOT

This is a valuable knot to fly anglers because with it they can quickly, yet securely, fasten a dropper line to a nylon monofilament leader. Thus two, three, four, or more flies may be fished simultaneously on different droppers connected to the leader.

To tie the Pendre Dropper Knot simply wind the end of the dropper line once around the nylon leader. Then wrap the dropper end three times around the standing part of the dropper line. Now insert the end through the first loop and the last loop. A Pendre Dropper Knot will tend to "slip" up or down a monofilament leader if the knot isn't tightened carefully.

(For more information on this knot, turn to page 44.)

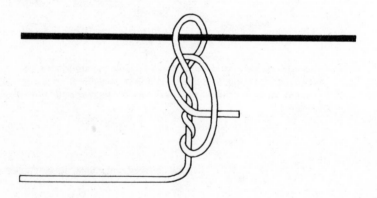

THE ANGLER'S KNOT (Also called Single Fishermen's Knot)

This is another way to tie in dropper lines for fishing two, three, four, or more flies at the same time.

The Angler's Knot is especially valuable to fly fishermen because it can be tied "on the stream" very quickly. However, because an Overhand Knot must be tied in the main leader to attach the dropper line, it reduces the rated pound test of the leader. Thus, this knot should only be used when it isn't practical to tie a better dropper knot, such as the Extension Blood Knot, or when small fish are being taken.

(For more information on this knot, turn to page 19.)

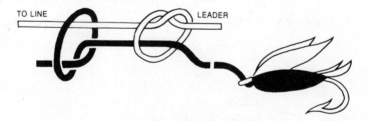

TO LINE   LEADER

Fig. 1 Lay the main leader and the dropper leader alongside each other. Make an Overhand Knot, with the main leader, around the dropper leader. Then make an Overhand Knot with the dropper line around the main leader. Pull on the standing part and tag end of each leader to tighten the two knots and "jam" them together.

A VARIATION OF THE NEEDLE KNOT

This is a faster, more easily tied knot than the Needle Nail Knot. Although it isn't as secure a tie as the Needle Knot, nonetheless the Variation Of The Needle Knot is a fine connection for light, fresh water fly fishing.

Some fly rodders choose this knot because the leader butt comes *directly from the center* of the fly line. They believe that causes the fly leader to lie straighter on the water.

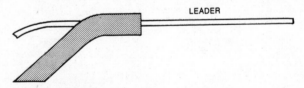

Fig. 1 Thread the leader butt through the "eye" of the needle. Push the needle through the center of the fly line, then out about one-half inch from the line end.

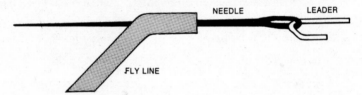

Fig. 2 This is how the knot should look thus far.

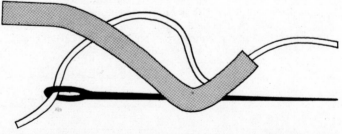

Fig. 3 Push the needle completely through the fly line a second time, one inch above the point where the needle passed through the line initially. Then insert the needle a third time—into and out of the fly line—as illustrated.

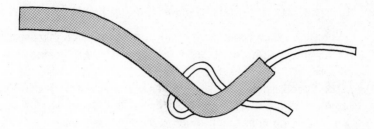

Fig. 4 At this stage the knot should look like this.

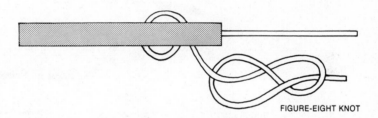

FIGURE-EIGHT KNOT

Fig. 5 Tie a Figure Eight Knot in the end of the leader butt.

Fig. 6 Pull on the standing part of the leader to draw the Variation Of The
Needle Knot tight.

BLOOD KNOT

The Blood Knot is the most widely used knot among fly fishermen for joining lengths of nylon monofilament when making tapered leaders.

The Blood Knot is easy to tie. It's extremely strong when made properly. Moreover, it is especially valuable to fly rodders because it is a small knot and runs through rod guides with ease.

Only monofilament of nearly equal diameters should be joined with the Blood Knot, to insure the greatest knot strength.

(For more information on this knot, turn to page 34.)

Fig. 1 Cross two sections of monofilament and wrap one section three or four times around the other. Now place the wrapped end through the loop formed by the two mono sections.

Fig. 2 Turn the other line around the standing part of the first line three or four times, and put its free end through the loop from the opposite side.

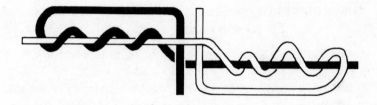

Fig. 3 At this stage the turns should look this way. Now slowly pull on both ends of the line.

Fig. 4 With its ends trimmed closely, the finished knot looks like this.

SURGEON'S KNOT (Occasionally called the Double Water Knot and Joiner Knot)

The Surgeon's Knot is used often by fly fishermen for joining a heavy "shock tippet" to the end of a leader.

A "shock tippet" of 60-, 80-, or 100-pound test nylon monofilament is a "must" when angling for toothy fish such as muskellunge, northern pike, barracuda, etc. Thus the knot-tying problem of connecting very heavy mono to a light (usually 12-pound test) nylon leader occurs often.

The one drawback to the Surgeon's Knot is that it can be difficult to "tighten." Unless all four ends of the knot are drawn together smoothly, slowly, and equally, the knot is difficult to tie.

(For more information on this knot, turn to page 25.)

SHOCK LEADER

TO REEL

Fig. 1 Form a Double Overhand Knot with the long end of the shock leader and the short, tag end of the line. Draw very tight.

TRIPLE FISHERMAN'S KNOT

Some fly rod anglers feel the Triple Fisherman's Knot is much stronger than the more conventional Blood Knot. Also, they believe it is easier to tie.

The Triple Fisherman's Knot is a good one for joining two pieces of monofilament when making a fly fishing leader. The knot is particularly useful in connecting two sections of leader material having different diameters.

(For more information on this knot, turn to page 38.)

Fig. 1 Wrap one end of nylon leader material three times around the standing part of another section of leader material. Bring the leader end back over the three wraps, then under the wraps, as shown. Make this same knot with the other leader end, onto the standing part of the first section of leader.

Fig. 2 Here's the finished Triple Fisherman's Knot after it's been tightened and trimmed.

FAST NAIL KNOT (Often called Instant Nail Knot, Speed Nail Knot, and 20 Second Nail Knot)

Many anglers dislike the standard Nail Knot, although the Nail Knot is best for joining mono leaders to fly lines. Such fishermen figure, and perhaps rightly so, that making a standard Nail Knot is difficult and certainly time consuming. However, the *Fast Nail Knot* is an easy, swift way to make a Nail Knot for connecting a leader butt to a fly line. The Fast Nail Knot cannot be used for attaching backing line to a fly line, because in tying this knot it's necessary to loop the line over itself. You can't do that when tying to backing.

The Fast Nail Knot can be made with a straightened paper clip, a toothpick, sliver of wood, nail, needle—anything that is straight and will provide some rigidity.

(For more information on this knot, turn to page 48.)

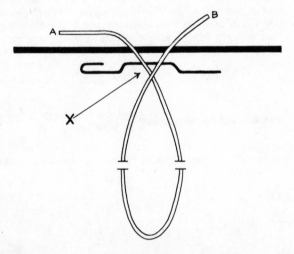

Fig. 1 Hold a paper clip (or similar rigid item) parallel to the fly line. Form a loop with the nylon monofilament, and lay it over the fly line and paper clip. "A" is the leader butt, "B" is the leader point, or tip. All components are held at point "X" with the thumb and forefinger of the left hand.

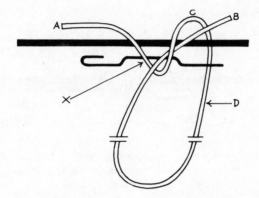

Fig. 2 Continue holding all components at "X," and with the right hand holding the mono leader at about "D," begin rolling the monofilament line over itself at "C." The mono is looped over itself, the flyline, and the paper clip.

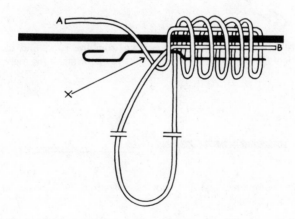

Fig. 3 Still holding at "X" with thumb and forefinger, wrap the mono around itself, the flyline, and the clip about six times.

FAST NAIL KNOT (continued)

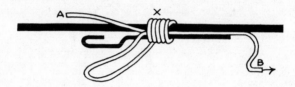

Fig. 4 Holding firmly at "X," pull the mono end "B" through on the right side of the knot until the knot tightens. Leader end "B" will lengthen as the mono (or leader) is pulled through the nail knot.

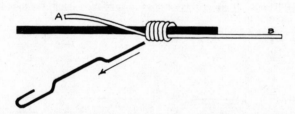

Fig. 5 Now the paper clip is withdrawn from the knot, and the knot is tightened by pulling on both "A" and "B" ends of the monofilament.

Fig. 6 The completed Fast Nail Knot looks like this after it has been trimmed and tightened.

KNOT FOR FASTENING LINE TO A FLY REEL

It isn't necessary for fly anglers to make an extremely secure connection between line and fly reel. If for any reason a fish takes all of the line from the fly reel—no knot on earth will hold him.

The knot illustrated is fast to tie and is adequate for the purpose.

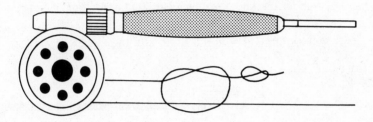

Fig. 1 Wrap the fly line or backing line once around the reel spool. Fasten a tight Overhand Knot at the end of the line. Tie another Overhand Knot with the line end over the standing part of the line. Tighten the knot and pull on the standing part of the line to "jam" the two knots against the fly reel spool.

NAIL KNOT (Sometimes referred to as Tube Knot)

The Nail Knot is undoubtedly one of the most useful knots to the fly fisherman. Although there are many variations of this popular, well-known tie, nonetheless the standard Nail Knot is the one most widely used.

It is used primarily for joining backing line to a fly line. However, some anglers still use the Nail Knot to join leader butts to fly lines, but the Fast Nail Knot is better suited for that purpose.

Many fishermen use a small tube or air pump needle, rather than a nail when tying a Nail Knot. They feel that it's easier to pass the mono line back under the knot's wraps when a tube or a hollow needle is employed.

(For more information on this knot, turn to page 36.)

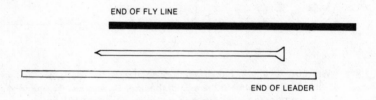

END OF FLY LINE

END OF LEADER

Fig. 1 Lay out the fly line and leader with the nail in between.

END OF FLY LINE

END OF LEADER

Fig. 2 Wrap the leader back toward the end of the fly line, making five tight turns, then pass its free end back through the center of the loops.

Fig. 3 This is how the knot should now look, with the nail still in place.

Fig. 4 Pull on both ends of the leader and fly line, and slowly withdraw the nail.

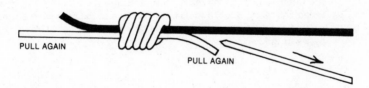

Fig. 5 Once the nail is removed, pull tightly on all four strands of line protruding from the knot.

Fig. 6 This is how the finished Nail Knot looks, with the two short ends trimmed close.

OVERHAND DROPPER TIE

The Overhand Dropper Tie is a very important "dropper knot" for all fly rodders. While it is not the most secure knot for tying in a dropper line, it can be tied very quickly.

(For more information on this knot, turn to page 33.)

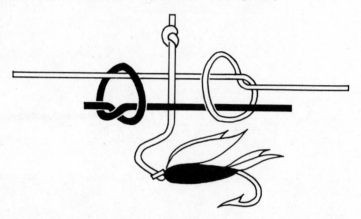

Fig. 1 Tie an Overhand Knot in the end of the dropper line. Then tie an Overhand Knot in one section of the main leader. Thread the end of the other section of the main leader through the Overhand Knot and tie an Overhand Knot in the second section of the main leader, going around the first main leader strand. Put the end of the dropper line between the two knots.

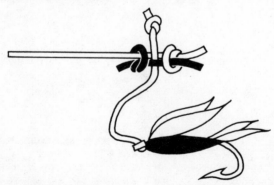

Fig. 2 The completed Overhand Dropper Tie after it's been tightened.

DROPPER SNELL KNOT

This is the fastest way to connect the line from a snelled fly to a leader for fly fishing. The Dropper Snell isn't as good as some other knots for attaching droppers, such as the Extension Blood Knot, but the Dropper Snell is adequate for most light, fresh water fly fishing.

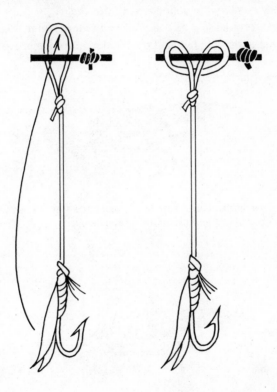

Fig. 1 Hold the loop of the dropper line at a right angle to the leader and bring the fly up through the loop in the dropper line.

Fig. 2 Pull on the dropper fly to tighten the knot. It's best to tie the Dropper Snell Knot just above a knot in the main leader to keep the Snell Knot from "sliding" down the leader.

THE END-LOOP KNOT (Sometimes called the Buffer Loop)

The End-Loop Knot is one of the better knots for attaching a fly to a heavy monofilament "shock tippet." The knot is fast and simple to tie, and is used often by fly rodders pursuing large or toothy game fish. The End-Loop Knot forms a loop through the "eye" of a fly, so the fly has life-like action when retrieved.

This knot should be used only with monofilament leaders that are so thick or stiff that it isn't practical to use an Improved Clinch Knot.

Fig. 1 Tie an Overhand Knot about six inches from the end of the line, then pass the line through the fly's hook eye.

Fig. 2 Put the line end through the open Overhand Knot and tie a Half-Hitch with the line end onto the standing part of the line.

Fig. 3 Slide the Overhand Knot either up or down the standing part of the line. This will determine the size of the loop that the knot will form. Slowly pull the line's end and its standing part to tighten the knot.

Fig. 4 Trim the knot, leaving a tag end about one-eighth inch long.

PORTLAND CREEK HITCH KNOT (Commonly called Riffling Hitch or Newfoundland Hitch)

No fly fisherman worth his waders should be on trout or salmon water without knowing how to tie this knot.

Many kinds of fish strike furiously at a fly that is activated on the surface. When a Portland Creek Hitch is tied to a fly, the leader draws away from the head of the fly at a 45 degree angle, causing the fly to "swim" and make a "V" wake on the water's surface. Such fly action sometimes is irresistible to salmon and trout.

When a fish strikes the fly, the "hitch" slips off the fly's head without knotting the leader.

The Portland Creek Hitch can be used effectively with certain streamers, grasshopper imitations, as well as with some dry fly patterns.

Fig. 1 Tie the leader to the fly with a reliable knot, such as a Turle Knot or an Improved Clinch Knot. Then tie a Half-Hitch with the leader and tighten it on the fly's head.

Fig. 2 Tighten the Half-Hitch so that the leader comes away at the bottom or side of the fly's head.

SHOCKER KNOT

Often a fly fisherman needs a heavy length of nylon monofilament at the end of his leader to act as a "shock tippet." For fish such as tarpon, snook, and northern pike, "shock tippets" of 60-pound mono or heavier are absolutely necessary if the angler wants to hold the fish he hooks.

The Shocker Knot is a very fast way to join a light leader (normally 12- or 15-pound test) to a piece of heavy nylon. Many experienced fly rodders consider the Shocker Knot much easier to tie than the Surgeon's Knot and, too, they consider it almost as strong.

(For more information on this knot, turn to page 18.)

Fig. 1 Make an Overhand Knot in the light leader. Form a loose Overhand Knot in the heavy leader material and pass the end of the light leader through the loose Overhand Knot.

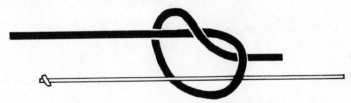

Fig. 2 Tighten the Overhand Knot in the shock leader.

Fig. 3 Make three wraps with the light leader around the heavy leader, then bring the end back through the first loop. Draw tight.

KNOTTING BACKING TO FLY LINE

Although this knot takes a little time to tie it is extremely secure and will pass through rod guides easily, which is important when fighting fish like bonefish and tarpon.

Fig. 1 Tie a simple Square Knot with the fly line and backing line.

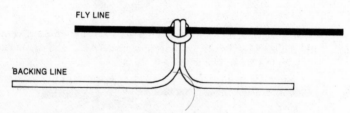

Fig. 2 Pull the fly line straight, and tug the backing line downward.

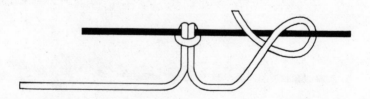

Fig. 3 Pull the Square Knot tight, and tie six Half-Hitches onto the fly line with the short end of the backing.

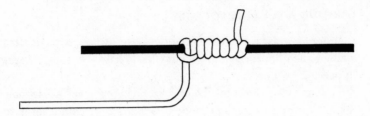

Fig. 4 Pull the Half-Hitches tight, and trim the short end of the backing line.

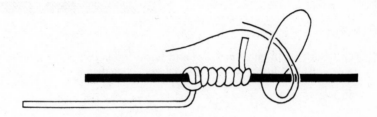

Fig. 5 Wrap the knot with nylon thread, and continue over the knot, wrapping the short end of the fly line to the backing line.

Fig. 6 After wrapping with nylon thread, coat the entire knot with Pliobond cement or lacquer.

FORMING A FLY LINE LOOP (II)

Although most fly rodders no longer use fly line loops to attach a leader to a fly line, or to join backing line to a fly line, some still prefer to use the Fly Line Loop.

If a loop in the line is desired, this is one of the best ways to make it. When this loop is made properly it is extremely strong, yet is small enough to pass through fly rod guides readily.

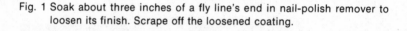

Fig. 1 Soak about three inches of a fly line's end in nail-polish remover to loosen its finish. Scrape off the loosened coating.

Fig. 2 Bend the cleaned fly line back to form a loop.

Fig. 3 Bind the looped lines tightly together using size 00 nylon thread, thus building a permanent loop. Lacquer or varnish the finished wrapping.

NEEDLE NAIL KNOT

This is an excellent knot for joining a leader to a fly line. The knot takes more time than a conventional Nail Knot, but some anglers believe their fly leaders lay straighter because the leader is attached to the center of the fly line.

Fig. 1 Push the needle through the blunt end of the fly line and out again about one-fourth inch from the end. Put the end of the leader through the needle eye, and pull the needle through the fly line, which will bring the nylon leader after it.

Fig. 2 Now tie a conventional Nail Knot, but use the needle instead of a nail. Make four to six wraps around the needle, then put the end of the leader through the needle eye.

Fig. 3 Now pull the needle through the knot, and the leader will follow.

Fig. 4 After the short leader end is trimmed, the finished knot looks like this.

IMPROVED CLINCH KNOT (Also known as Pandre Knot or Jam Knot
With An Extra Tuck)

The Improved Clinch Knot is considered by veteran fly fishermen
to be the strongest knot for attaching flies to leaders ranging from
light to medium heavy.

The Improved Clinch Knot can be tied very quickly, even at night,
and it forms only a small, nicely straight connection at the hook eye.

When using heavy leader tippets (40 pounds or more), it isn't
practical to use the Improved Clinch Knot. It is difficult to tighten this
knot with heavy mono, so another knot, such as the regular Clinch
Knot, or the End Loop Knot, should be employed. Moistening the
Improved Clinch Knot with saliva will help tighten it.

Fig. 1 Pass the end of the line through the hook eye. Put about six inches of
line through the eye so there will be ample line with which to tie the
knot.

Fig. 2 Hold the fly securely in one hand and wrap the end of the line five times around the standing part of the line, as shown in the illustration. Now pass the end of the line back through the small loop near the hook eye, and also through the large loop.

Fig. 3 The finished Improved Clinch Knot—tightened and trimmed.

TWO CIRCLE TURLE KNOT

This is an improved version of the regular Turle Knot. It may be a little more difficult to tie, but it is stronger.

The Two Circle Turle Knot was designed for tying flies with turned-up or turned-down "eyes" to monofilament leaders. It is an excellent knot, particularly when used with dry flies, because it helps the fly to ride higher in the water.

Fig. 1 Put the leader end through the hook eye, and slide the fly up the leader out of the way. Form a loop with the leader about six inches from the end.

Fig. 2 Make a second loop, and overlay the two.

Fig. 3 Now tie an Overhand Knot over the two loops, and tighten the Overhand Knot.

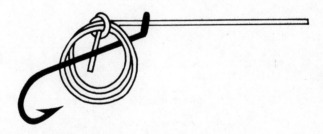

Fig. 4 Pass the fly through the two loops.

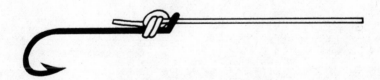

Fig. 5 Pull on the leader end and its standing part until the knot tightens behind the fly's hook eye. The completed Two Circle Turle Knot is shown.

One way to remove kinks from a nylon monofilament leader is to draw it repeatedly across a rubber shoe sole.

6 Wire, Cable Connections

Heavy nylon monofilament certainly is the best leader material for most fresh water and salt water fishing. However, for some fishing, wire must be used. Wire line is often used in deep trolling, and wire leaders are used not infrequently by fishermen after northern pike and muskies. More appropriately, wire leaders are used in much offshore fishing, for taking toothy fish such as sharks, barracuda, king fish, mackerel, etc.

Generally, there are three types of wire leaders—nylon-coated wire cable, single-strand stainless steel, and wire cable. Tying knots with any of them, or connecting fishing lines to them, presents some very difficult and unique problems.

Most of the knots and connections that can be employed with ordinary fishing lines and leaders cannot be used with wire. Wire is too stiff, and has too much tendency to kink. Fortunately, many special wire "wraps" have been developed over the years that hold well, even under the extreme pressures exerted by large ocean game fish.

HAY-WIRE TWIST

This is one of the best ways to link solid wire to any type of connecting ring. The number of wraps and the two different kinds of wraps in the Hay-wire Twist may seem elaborate to many fishermen, but for numerous varieties of salt water fish this tie is absolutely necessary to keep the wire from "pulling out."

Fig. 1 Thread the end of the wire through the hook eye, pulling about five inches of wire through the "eye."

Fig. 2 Bend the end of the wire back over its standing part, forming a small loop.

Fig. 3 Wrap the end of the wire over the standing part of the wire about six or seven times. Then hold the standing part of the wire straight out from the hook eye, and wrap the wire end tightly around it six times at a 90 degree angle.

Fig. 4 Bend the tag end of the wire back and forth until it breaks, and the Hay-wire Twist is completed.

RIG FOR CUT BAIT

This is an elaborate method of fastening a hook with a wire leader for use in trolling cut bait for large game fish. It is an excellent, strong rig.

The wire is inserted through the hook eye and wrapped around the hook shank six or seven times. Then its end is brought back out the hook eye, and a standard Hay-wire Twist is made. The tag end of the wire is left protruding from the Hay-wire Twist like a "pin." This "pin" is used to keep the cut bait secured to the hook.

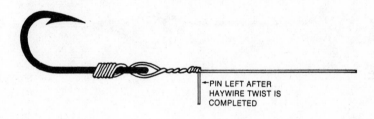

←PIN LEFT AFTER
HAYWIRE TWIST IS
COMPLETED

SINGLE-SLEEVE RIG

To rig this connection thread wire through a metal sleeve, pass the wire through the hook eye, then back through the sleeve. Crimp the sleeve and trim the tag end of the wire.

The Single-Sleeve Rig is one of the most popular ways of connecting wire to a hook eye or to a lure. It is commonly used by salt water anglers for light "inshore" fishing.

(Wire and metal sleeves are obtainable at most tackle shops.)

JOINING WIRE TO BRAIDED LINE

This connection is used by anglers, when fishing for toothy fish such as barracuda, who want to tie wire leaders to braided bait-casting line.

This knot can be difficult to make because the wire tends to kink unless the tie is made with the utmost care.

WIRE

Fig. 1 Tie a loop in the end of the braided line (use the Spider Hitch or the Perfection Loop). Put the end of the wire through the loop and wrap the end around one side of the loop.

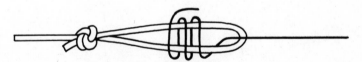

Fig. 2 Wind the wire completely around the loop twice.

Fig. 3 Bring the wire back out through the loop, and wrap it four times around the standing part of the wire.

OVERHAND WIRE WRAP (Occasionally called Barrel Twist)

This is merely the second part of the Hay-wire Twist. The wire end is put through the hook eye and wrapped around the standing part of the wire four or five times at a 90 degree angle.

The Overhand Wire Wrap is a fine connection for use in light salt water fishing. However, when large fish may be encountered a Hay-wire Twist or a Single-Sleeve Rig is usually preferred.

METAL SLEEVE SECURING A LOOP OF WIRE

This is another variation of the Single-Sleeve Rig. It can be used to connect wire to a hook or lure "eye," or it can be used to form a simple wire loop to which a leader or line may be attached.

Fig. 1 Pass the wire through the sleeve and double the wire back toward the sleeve.

Fig. 2 Put the wire through the sleeve again, leaving whatever size loop is desired.

Fig. 3 Turn the end of the wire back into the sleeve.

Fig. 4 Crimp the sleeve firmly and the connection is finished.

QUICK-CHANGE WIRE WRAP

The Quick-Change Wire Wrap is the perfect connection for anglers who need a wire wrap for use with light tackle, yet want the convenience of being able to change lures quickly.

Although this wire wrap is not as strong as some other wire connections, such as the Hay-wire Twist, it is adequate for most light salt water angling.

The trick to making the Quick-Change Wire Wrap is to make the ''wraps'' of the wire end onto the standing part of the wire somewhat apart. The wide wraps make the tie much stronger than if ''tight'' wraps were used.

Also, because the wraps are made far apart, the connection is easy to unravel. Thus a lure can be put on or taken off very quickly.

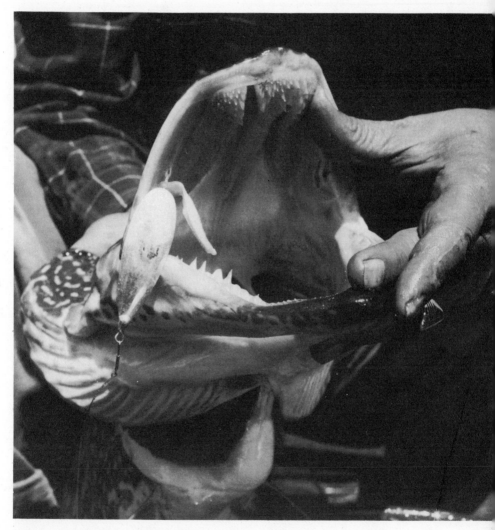

Large canine teeth, and rows of smaller teeth on palate and tongue, make wire leaders practical in fishing for northern pike. Special connections are needed to link wire to line, snaps, etc.

SAFETY-PIN RIG

The Safety-Pin Rig is an excellent way of attaching wire to a large hook for use in trolling "strip baits."

The wire should be threaded through the hook eye. Four large wraps are made around the standing part of the wire, followed by five or six "tight" wraps. At this point the wrap will look something like a Hay-wire Twist.

The final step is bending the wire end straight up from the standing part of the wire, bending it again at a right angle to the standing part, and then bending a small U-shape into the wire's end.

Bending the wire is done easiest with needle-nose pliers.

SAFETY PIN MADE WITH
WIRE LEADER

METAL SLEEVE AND KNOT

This is a superb connection for joining heavy wire or cable to a hook. The Metal Sleeve And Knot is adequate for most types of salt water trolling. However, this is a permanent tie that is most practical when used with trolling outfits that will not be "broken down" after each day's use.

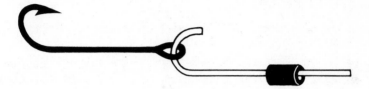

Fig. 1 Thread the wire through the sleeve and hook eye.

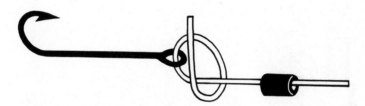

Fig. 2 Wrap the end of the wire around the standing part of the wire.

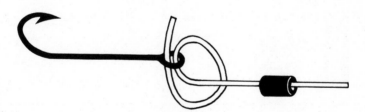

Fig. 3 Pass the end through the hook eye again.

Fig. 4 Now bring the wire end through the open loop, through the sleeve, crimp the sleeve tight, and trim the excess wire.

DOUBLE-SLEEVE RIG

This connection is slightly more elaborate than a Single-Sleeve Rig, however, the Double-Sleeve Rig is much stronger. For that reason, it is favored by many anglers for attaching cable to large hooks for offshore trolling.

To make this connection, insert wire through two sleeves. Pass the end through the hook eye, then back through one sleeve. Now wrap the wire end once around the standing part of the wire, and push the end through the second sleeve. Crimp both sleeves and trim the excess wire end.

KNOTTING NYLON-COATED WIRE TO MONO LINE

Many veteran anglers believe that this is the best, most secure knot for tying nylon-coated wire line to nylon monofilament line.

It's important when tying this knot to keep the wire line straight while the knot is being pulled tight. This will keep the wire from kinking when the "wraps" of nylon mono are drawn together.

WIRE   MONO

Fig. 1 Form a loop with the wire line and a loop with the mono line. Place the two loops on top of each other, as shown.

Fig. 2 Wrap the monofilament line six times around the wire loop. Then insert the mono end through the wire loop.

Fig. 3 To tighten the knot, slowly pull on the standing parts of both the mono and wire lines.

Fig. 4 The finished knot.

SPECIAL SPOON WRAP (Sometimes referred to as Trolling Spoon Wrap)

This is an excellent way of attaching wire to a spoon or other artificial lure. The Special Spoon Wrap forms a wire loop through the lure's connecting ring and allows the lure to "swim" more life like.

This wire connection is used by many salt water fishing guides for such fish as king mackerel. And, too, it is used by many northern anglers in deep trolling for lake trout.

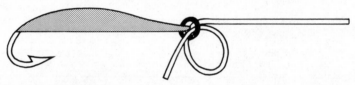

Fig. 1 Put the end of the wire through a lure's connecting hole or ring twice, leaving about four or five inches of wire with which to make the wrap.

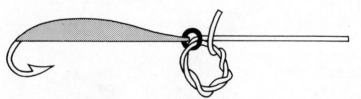

Fig. 2 Wrap the wire end four times around the wire circle formed through the lure's connecting ring.

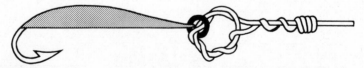

Fig. 3 Wind the wire end loosely around the standing part of the wire twice, then make several tight wraps around the standing wire, similar to the way a Hay-wire Twist is made.

FIGURE EIGHT KNOT

Although the Figure Eight Knot is recommended only in emergency situations when used with nylon monofilament or braided lines, it is an extremely secure tie when used with braided wire.

The Figure Eight Knot is employed often by anglers using braided wire line while deep "jigging" for toothy species of fish.

(For more information on this knot, turn to page 27.)

Fig. 1 Put the wire end through the hook or lure "eye." Bring the end back and wind it once around the standing part of the wire, then insert the end through the loop formed in front of the hook eye.

Fig. 2 The Figure Eight Knot after it has been drawn tight.

BALAO RIG (Also called Ballyhoo Rig)

This is the standard method for rigging a hook with wire when trolling offshore with a balao bait.

It's quite easy to prepare this rig. First, affix a small, seven-inch piece of wire to the hook eye with an Overhand Wire Wrap. Then attach a wire leader to the hook eye with a Hay-wire Twist.

It's important to leave a small one-half inch tag end of wire after the Hay-wire Twist is completed. With a pair of pliers bend the Hay-wire Twist tag end of wire at a right angle to the standing part of the wire leader. This tag end of the wire is used to help hold the balao bait on the hook.

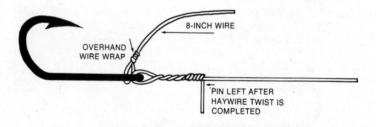

CIRCLE WRAP WITH DOUBLE SLEEVE (Also known as Big Game Cable Loop)

This is *the* connection to use when securing multistrand aircraft cable to a hook for big game trolling. This wrap, when properly made, will withstand the tremendous stresses that the largest marlin or tuna can cause.

To make the connection, insert the cable or wire through two metal sleeves and then through the hook eye twice, forming a small, one-half inch diameter loop. Wrap the wire end around the loop four times, then insert the end of the wire through the first sleeve, and crimp the sleeve. Wind the wire end twice around the standing part of the wire, insert the end through the second sleeve and crimp it.

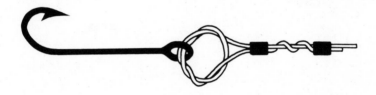

THE MATCH METHOD (Also called Heated Twist)

This is the quickest way to secure a lure or hook to nylon-coated wire, and when properly done it is a very durable, strong connection.

The Match Method is easy. Merely push the end of the nylon-coated wire through the hook, lure, or swivel "eye." Then make five twists around the standing part of the wire with the end of the wire. Now light a match and pass it back and forth quickly along the wraps of the wire. When the nylon coating begins to fuse, remove the match. After the nylon cools, the connection is complete.

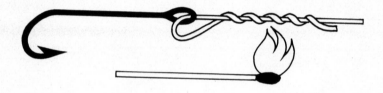

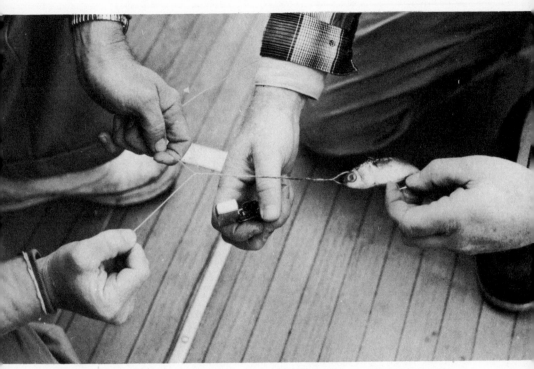

Flame from cigarette lighter melts nylon on coated wire, fuses the strands.

7 Knots in Everyday Fishing

Knowing how to tie knots is a skill needed by every fisherman. However, if the fisherman does not know how to apply his knot-tying knowledge, if he does not understand when and where to employ specific knots in rigging different tackle, then his knot-tying expertise is of little value.

This chapter presents concrete examples of how to use acceptable knots in "everyday" fishing situations

The knots shown in the following fishing rigs were selected because they are commonly used by most experts. However, there is duplication of purpose in many knots, and while a Bimini Twist may be shown as performing one function, a Spider Hitch could readily be substituted.

Usually more than one kind of knot is needed when putting together any fishing rig. This chapter illustrates the different knots that can be used with various fishing rigs.

HEAVY-DUTY FLY LEADER

Some of the same knots are used in making up this leader as are used in making a Light, Fresh Water Fly Leader, but different lengths and tests of nylon monofilament are necessary in making a Heavy-Duty Fly Leader. This leader is excellent for fish such as tarpon, snook, barracuda, northern pike, and muskellunge. Note, however, that the "shock tippet" may range from 30- to 100-pound test.

A Fast Nail Knot (or other type Nail Knot) should be used to secure the permanent butt section of the leader to the fly line. Then all the other leader sections are joined with Blood Knots. The "shock tippet" is connected to the 12-pound test nylon with a Shocker Knot. The Shocker Knot is used because it is an excellent knot for tying two pieces of mono together that are of different diameters. The Homer Rhode Loop is used at the fly because it can be tied readily with heavy nylon. Too, the "loop" it forms through the fly's hook eye permits the best possible action of the fly when it's retrieved.

RIGGING A MULLET FOR DEEP TROLLING

Most skilled salt water anglers are familiar with this rig. It is an excellent way to present a bait to billfish when trolling offshore.

The backbone of the mullet is removed with a deboning tool and the entrails are removed. This gives the bait more action in the water.

The hook is positioned in the cut in the mullet's belly so the hook eye is just inside its mouth. A two- or four-ounce "egg" sinker is threaded with wire leader, and the wire end is then pushed up through the fish's lower jaw, through the hook eye, and finally out the top of the fish's head. A Hay-wire Twist is put in the wire.

The final step is to take a heavy-duty needle and stout thread, and sew the fish's mouth and its slit belly, closed.

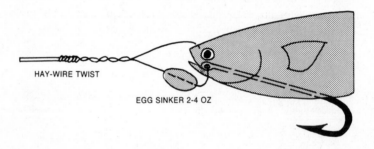

HAY-WIRE TWIST

EGG SINKER 2-4 OZ

DEEP TROLLING SPOON RIG WITH A WIRE LEADER

This rigging is used by Great Lakes anglers who want to get a trolled spoon or lure down deep while fishing for lake trout and salmon. It also is popular among some "inshore" salt water anglers. The wire leader helps keep the rig down, and fish with sharp teeth can't cut it.

To make this outfit attach a pinch-on sinker about one foot from the end of the fishing line, and slip a "trolling keel" onto the line (the trolling keel helps prevent line twist).

Attach a barrel swivel to the end of the fishing line with an Offshore Swivel Knot. Next connect the wire leader to the swivel with an Overhand Wire Wrap, which is adequate for most light trolling situations. Use the Special Spoon Wrap to fasten the spoon to the wire. The Special Spoon Wrap will enable the spoon to wobble freely and life-like while being trolled.

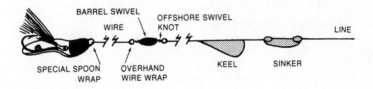

BOTTOM RIG FOR SURF FISHING

This bottom bait fishing rig is common on all three coasts. A six-ounce pyramid sinker will hold well in most surf, but a larger sinker can be used if necessary. The rig is employed often by anglers after fish such as striped bass and channel bass, since those fish frequent strong surf and areas with heavy current.

Usually heavy line is needed for casting and fishing in the surf, because large sinkers are used to hold the bait on the bottom. For this reason, the Jansik Special is the perfect knot for securing the fishing line to the three-way swivel. The Jansik Special is a very strong knot and is easy to tie with heavy monofilament.

A loop should be formed in the leader that runs to the sinker and connected to the three-way swivel with a Lark's Head Knot. The Lark's Head Knot can be tied quickly and it holds well. The other end of the heavy leader is connected to the pyramid sinker "eye" with a Jansik Special.

Finally, a hook is snelled to a leader, a loop formed at the other end of the leader, and the loop then connected to the three-way swivel with a Lark's Head Knot.

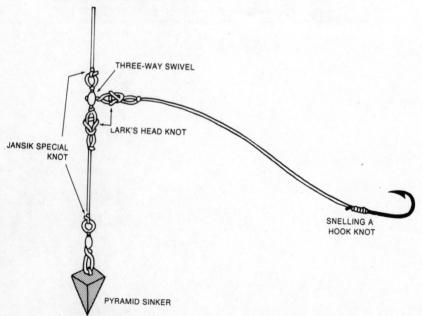

THREE-WAY SWIVEL

LARK'S HEAD KNOT

JANSIK SPECIAL KNOT

SNELLING A HOOK KNOT

PYRAMID SINKER

RIGGING A NYLON "SHOCK LEADER"

This rig is one of the most popular for tying a "shock leader" to braided or nylon monofilament line.

When a "shock leader" is needed for certain types of fishing, the first thing that should be done is to form a doubled line at the end of the fishing line (a doubled line assures 100 percent efficiency from the knots). The Spider Hitch is a superb knot for creating a doubled line.

The heavy, monofilament "shock leader" then should be tied to the doubled line with an Albright Special. Finally, the lure is connected to the heavy nylon with a Homer Rhode Loop. This knot can be tied easily with heavy nylon, and it allows a lure to "swim" more life-like than if the mono were tied tightly to the lure's connecting ring.

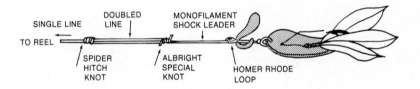

SINGLE LINE — DOUBLED LINE — MONOFILAMENT SHOCK LEADER — TO REEL — SPIDER HITCH KNOT — ALBRIGHT SPECIAL KNOT — HOMER RHODE LOOP

RIGGING TWO LURES ON A THREE-WAY SWIVEL

This is a fine rig for fishing two lures simultaneously. Usually a surface lure, or a floating-diving lure, is used in conjunction with a deep-running lure—such as a lead-head jig. When the rig is retrieved, the two lures travel at different depths, and their leaders are unlikely to tangle.

This three-way swivel rig also is used by anglers fishing for "school fish," such as crappies and white bass. Many times when one fish is hooked another will strike the second lure as it is pulled through the water by the first fish.

Both lures should be tied to the leaders with a Dave Hawk's Drop-Loop Knot. This is a good, strong, easy-to-tie knot that will permit both lures to vibrate and wiggle freely.

All three lines tied to the three-way swivel should be knotted with an Eye-Crosser Knot. The Eye-Crosser Knot has excellent knot strength and is quickly made.

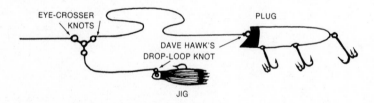

RIGGING A BALAO FOR TROLLING

The balao, which is a small beakfish, is considered one of the best natural baits for billfish.

Rigging A Balao For Trolling is quite different from preparing any other type of bait for trolling. First, the hook should be prepared with the special Balao Rig, as shown. Then the hook should be placed in the balao (see illustration). Be sure the wire "pin" left on the Hay-wire Twist is pushed through the top of the balao's head, and the short piece of wire leader should be wound tightly around the fish's beak.

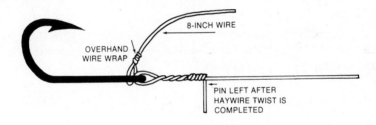

8-INCH WIRE

OVERHAND
WIRE WRAP

PIN LEFT AFTER
HAYWIRE TWIST IS
COMPLETED

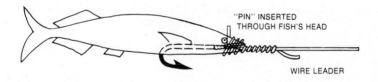

"PIN" INSERTED
THROUGH FISH'S HEAD

WIRE LEADER

RIGGING A NYLON LEADER TO BRAIDED LINE

This is the way many bait casters attach a nylon monofilament leader to braided casting line. The rig is good for light or medium-heavy fresh or salt water angling.

A loop is formed at one end of the mono leader with a Perfection Loop Knot. Then the braided line is joined to the loop with a Multiple Clinch Knot. An Improved Clinch Knot should be used to attach the mono leader to a snap swivel, and the lure then is snapped to the swivel.

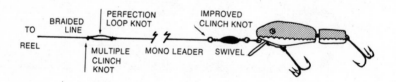

NEW ZEALAND OFFSHORE TROLLING RIG

Few big game, offshore salt water anglers use this trolling rig. Yet it's a good one and it can be made very quickly.

First a large hook is "sewn" to the jaws of a natural bait, such as a bonefish or mackerel. After each wrap around the hook's bend a Half-Hitch should be made with the twine.

Finally, the hook is linked to the wire leader with a Hay-wire Twist.

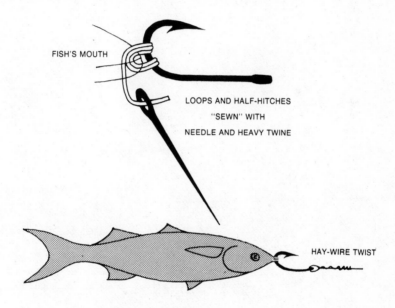

FISH'S MOUTH

LOOPS AND HALF-HITCHES
"SEWN" WITH
NEEDLE AND HEAVY TWINE

HAY-WIRE TWIST

A bluefin tuna is hoisted up the gin pole aboard the "Dream Girl," fishing off Bimini. When records are at stake, or tournament wins, terminal rigging is ultra important.

SPREADER RIG FOR NATURAL BAITS

This natural bait rig can be used for many kinds of fresh and salt water fish.

The first thing to do when making this rig is to purchase a wire "spreader" of a size most suitable to the type of fishing to be done.

Bait rigs of this sort frequently become foul hooked on bottom. Because of this, the Double Loop Improved Clinch Knot should be used when tying the fishing line to the center swivel "eye" of the "spreader," and also when connecting the two nylon monofilament leaders to the "spreader."

The Double Loop Improved Clinch Knot will hold up very well under the stresses caused by pulling heavily on the line to free bottom-fouled hooks.

Both bait hooks should be joined to the two leaders with the Snelling A Hook Knot. Snelled hook knots are very strong and they give a good direct pull from line to hook, which is essential for consistent hooking of fish.

The sinker in this rigging is joined to a light leader with the Loop For Attaching A Single "Eye" Sinker. The sinker leader then is tied to the "spreader" with a Figure Eight Knot, because this weak knot will break should the sinker "hang up" on the bottom. If a break occurs, only the sinker is lost—not the entire rig.

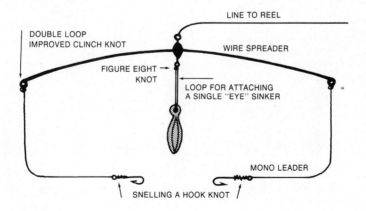

STRIP-BAIT TROLLING RIG

Although there are numerous ways to rig strip or "cut" baits for offshore trolling, many expert salt water anglers consider this one the best. The rig is strong, allows the bait to have plenty of "action" in the water, and it can be made quickly.

To prepare this rig, first connect the fishing line to a heavy-duty swivel, using an Improved Clinch Knot. Then, join one end of a seven-foot wire trolling leader to the swivel with a Hay-wire Twist. Finally, fasten the wire leader end to the hook with a Safety-Pin Rig, then attach the strip bait.

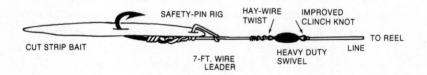

CUT STRIP BAIT SAFETY-PIN RIG HAY-WIRE TWIST IMPROVED CLINCH KNOT TO REEL LINE 7-FT. WIRE LEADER HEAVY DUTY SWIVEL

POPPING CORK RIG

The Popping Cork Rig is excellent when angling for fish such as sea trout, snook, and red fish (channel bass). The cork is a specially designed float. It is "popped" by the angler (when he raises his rod tip sharply), and such commotion attracts game fish to the jig or other lure attached below the popping cork. The cork also can signal strikes to the angler.

To make this rig, attach a popping cork about one foot from the end of the fishing line. Join the end of the line to a barrel swivel with the strong, simple-to-tie, Improved Clinch Knot.

Next, use the Crawford Knot to join a heavy "shock tippet" to the other end of the barrel swivel. A "shock tippet" is needed when after fish with sharp teeth or gill covers, and the Crawford Knot is excellent for tying heavy monofilament securely.

Finally, use the Bob McNally Loop to tie a jig or other lure to the "shock tippet." This loop is not difficult to make with heavy line, yet it has good knot strength.

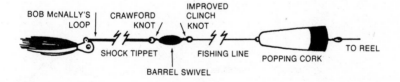

TROLLING RIG WITH A MONOFILAMENT LEADER

This rig can be made in just a few minutes. It is used most often by fresh water anglers trolling deep for fish such as walleyes, large-mouth and smallmouth bass, and northern pike.

Trolled lures frequently "hang up" on bottom. The advantage to this rig is that the dipsey sinker usually will "hang up" and not the lure. Because the sinker is tied to the three-way swivel with a weak Figure Eight Knot and a length of line lighter than the fishing line, the line to the sinker will break—not the line connecting the lure.

In making up this rig, the fishing line is fastened to a three-way swivel with a Double-Loop Clinch Knot. A short piece of monofila-ment line is tied to another ring of the three-way swivel, and to a barrel swivel, using Double-Loop Clinch Knots. Double-Loop Clinch Knots are used because they have excellent knot strength, which is absolutely necessary for this trolling rig.

A Nail Loop is used to tie the lure to the monofilament leader. The Nail Loop is a superb "loop knot," it's easy to tie with monofilament testing up to about 40 pounds, and it allows a lure to have the best possible action when trolled. The dipsey sinker is fastened to the three-way swivel with a short piece of light monofilament, and Figure Eight Knots are used.

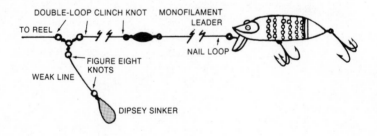

SALT WATER DEEP TROLLING RIG

This rig is used primarily for trolling natural baits, such as mullet or balao, over reefs for "bottom hugging" fish. However, a spoon or jig can be used rather than natural baits.

To make this rig, tie a permanent doubled line at the end of the braided fishing line, using the durable, Bimini Twist. (The doubled line will guarantee 100 percent knot strength in the line-to-wire connection.)

Tie a three foot length of wire to the doubled line with the Joining Wire To Braided Line knot, and fasten the other end of wire to a heavy, six-ounce trolling sinker with a Hay-wire Twist.

Next, join a six foot piece of wire to the other end of the trolling sinker, using a Hay-wire Twist, and attach the opposite end of the wire to a large hook with a Double-Sleeve Rig. Both the Hay-wire Twist and the Double-Sleeve Rig are superb connections to use with wire.

BRAIDED FISHING LINE   WIRE   HAY-WIRE TWIST   WIRE

BIMINI TWIST   JOINING WIRE TO BRAIDED LINE KNOT   6-OZ. TROLLING SINKER   DOUBLE-SLEEVE RIG

LIGHT, FRESH WATER FLY LEADER

Few anglers know how to make a fly leader properly. The fly leader is extremely important both for casting and presenting a fly to fish. In the illustration the length and pound test of each section of leader is shown for the best construction of a fresh water leader.

A Fast Nail Knot is used to tie the permanent leader butt to the fly line because it is the quickest, easiest Nail Knot to tie and, too, it goes through rod guides readily. The lengths of leader material are joined with Blood Knots. The Blood Knot is simple to tie, is strong, and makes a small connection. The Extension Blood Knot, although it takes more time to tie than some other knots, is the most dependable for attaching "dropper leaders" so that more than one fly can be fished simultaneously. And, finally, the Improved Clinch Knot is an excellent knot for tying a light nylon monofilament leader to a fly.

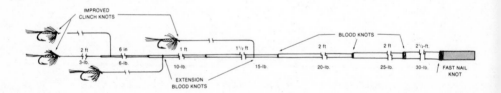

OFFSHORE WIRE LEADER

To make this rig, first form a double line with the fishing line by making the strong, easily-tied Spider Hitch. Then connect the doubled line to a heavy-duty barrel swivel, using a Palomar Knot. (This knot is recommended because it is easy to tie with a doubled line, yet is very strong.) Join the desired length of wire to the hook and to the swivel "eye" with a Hay-wire Twist.

Wire leaders of this type are used frequently by salt water bait-casting anglers when fishing for barracuda, etc.

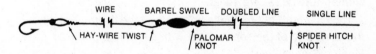

WIRE   BARREL SWIVEL   DOUBLED LINE   SINGLE LINE

HAY-WIRE TWIST   PALOMAR KNOT   SPIDER HITCH KNOT

COAT HANGER BAIT RIG FOR "REEF FISHING"

This is an old and reliable bait rig to use when bottom fishing for fish such as grouper, snappers, and amberjack. Different versions of this rig can be adapted according to the kind and size of fish sought and to the ocean's current and bottom conditions. The value of the Coat Hanger Bait Rig is that a live bait can be fished at any depth without it tangling with the sinker or fishing line.

The rig isn't as difficult to make as the illustration might indicate. First take the fishing line and make a doubled line, using the Double Line Loop. Then tie the doubled line to a heavy-duty snap swivel with a Double Improved Clinch Knot, and coat both knots with rubber cement.

The next step is to rig the coat hanger. Pinch the two ends of a coat hanger closed with pliers, and wrap them tightly with wire. Then, with the pliers, bend the hanger "neck" into a tight loop.

Attach a 10- or 12-foot wire leader to one end of the coat hanger, using a Hay-wire Twist. Run the wire through the loop made in the coat-hanger "neck," and fasten the bait hook to the end of the wire with another Hay-wire Twist.

Take a length of line that's lighter than the fishing line, and tie it to the other end of the coat hanger with a Figure Eight Knot, as shown. Make a Single Overhand Loop in the opposite end of the light-test line, and fasten the loop to a heavy "bank" sinker, using the Loop For Attaching A Single "Eye" Sinker.

Hook the live bait through the jaws, attach the snap swivel on the fishing line to the end of the coat hanger—and the rig is ready for fishing!

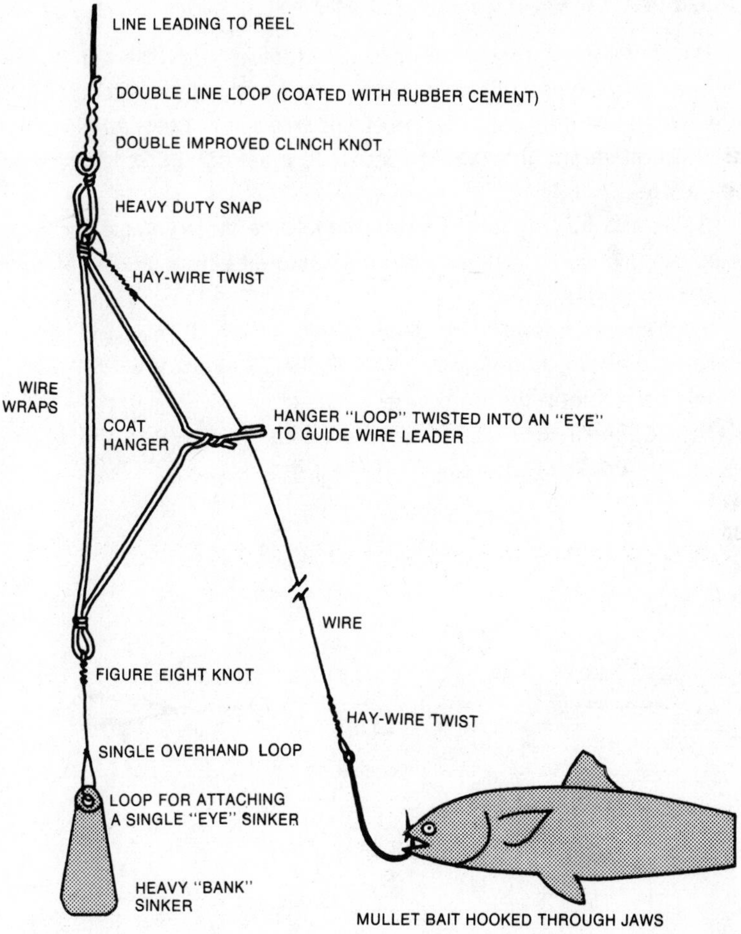

LINE LEADING TO REEL

DOUBLE LINE LOOP (COATED WITH RUBBER CEMENT)

DOUBLE IMPROVED CLINCH KNOT

HEAVY DUTY SNAP

HAY-WIRE TWIST

WIRE WRAPS

COAT HANGER

HANGER "LOOP" TWISTED INTO AN "EYE" TO GUIDE WIRE LEADER

WIRE

FIGURE EIGHT KNOT

HAY-WIRE TWIST

SINGLE OVERHAND LOOP

LOOP FOR ATTACHING A SINGLE "EYE" SINKER

HEAVY "BANK" SINKER

MULLET BAIT HOOKED THROUGH JAWS

PLUG WITH A SMALL TRAILING SPOON

When fishing is tough, it's often productive to try this rig, fishing two different types of lures simultaneously. A large surface plug is tied to the fishing line, and a small spoon or jig is attached to a piece of monofilament that's tied to the connecting ring of the larger plug's rear hook.

By fishing this rig, you may be able to determine what size or type lure the fish want, at what depth the fish are feeding, and what color lure they prefer.

The Duncan Loop should be used to tie the large plug and smaller lure to the two monofilament fishing lines. Each lure will "swim" freely on the loop during the retrieve.

The Clinch Knot is an adequate tie for connecting the trailing leader to the rear hook ring on the plug.

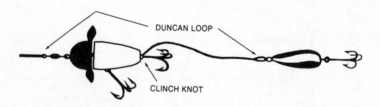

FEATHER-STRIP TROLLING RIG

The Feather-Strip Trolling Rig is deadly for many species of salt water gamefish. The rig combines the fish-attracting qualities of a feather head and the "smell" of a natural bait cut into strips.

The rig is simple to put together. Make a Hay-wire Twist at one end of a six foot wire leader, and connect the Hay-wire Twist to the monofilament fishing line with an Albright Special Knot. Next, pass the wire leader end through the hole in the feather head. Join the hook to the wire leader with the Rig For Cut Bait, and attach the strip bait as shown in the illustration.

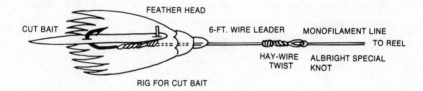

8 Splicing Lines

The method of connecting lines known as "splicing" is employed by comparatively few fishermen, and then only for special purposes. Most fishermen use a line-to-line knot, rather than a splice, to connect two lines.

There is an advantage to splicing lines, however, in that when properly done splicing provides a very small, smooth connection—one that will slip through rod guides much easier than a bulky knot.

SPLICED LOOP

Few fly fishermen still form a fly line loop this way, since the fly line coating is not removed from the actual loop and therefore the loop is bulkier than others. However, the Spliced Loop is extremely strong when properly tied.

Fig. 1 Remove one inch of the fly line coating from the end of the line, and also one inch of coating three inches from the end of the line. This can be done with nail-polish remover.

Fig. 2 Form the loop, and with size 00 nylon thread tightly wrap over the two pieces of fly line that have had the coating removed. Varnish or lacquer the completed splice.

CROTCH SPLICE

Although this splice takes some time to do, it is very secure for joining two fly lines or even for splicing braided lines.

Fig. 1 Use a pin or needle to fray the ends of the two lines. Fray about one inch of each line.

Fig. 2 Fork the frayed ends of both lines as shown. And then push the two "crotches" of each frayed end together.

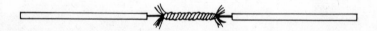

Fig. 3 Wind the splice tightly with heavy nylon thread and tie off. Cut the loose ends of the protruding fibers.

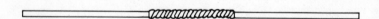

Fig. 4 Continue wrapping the splice with nylon thread until it looks like this. Coat splices with lacquer or Pliobond cement.

ROLLING SPLICE

This is not the easiest splice to learn for joining backing line to a fly line. However, it is one of the most secure.

The Rolling Splice can be made by one person, but it's much easier if an assistant holds the free end of the fly line, while the first person actually makes the splice.

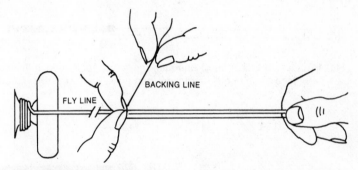

Fig. 1 Tie the fly line loosely to a door knob, leaving about two feet of line to work with. Lay the backing next to the fly line, and begin wrapping three inches from the end of the fly line. Wind the backing tightly onto the fly line, and wrap to within one-fourth inch from the end of the fly line.

Fig. 2 Now lay in a piece of fine nylon thread, and continue wrapping over the fly line and onto the backing line. Complete the splice with a whip finish by putting the end of the backing line in the nylon thread loop, pulling the two free ends of the thread. This will draw the backing line out in a reverse direction and secure the wrapping perfectly.

Fig. 3 This is how the finished splice looks after the loose ends have been trimmed. Pliobond cement or varnish may be applied if desired.

QUICK FLY LINE SPLICE

This splice is particularly popular among tournament casters who design their own shooting-head fly lines. The splice is easier to tie than it looks, and makes a good permanent connection.

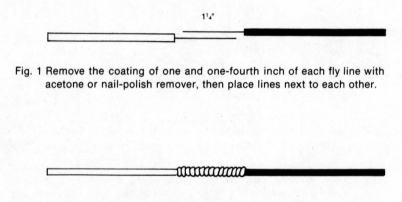

Fig. 1 Remove the coating of one and one-fourth inch of each fly line with acetone or nail-polish remover, then place lines next to each other.

Fig. 2 With nylon thread, wind the two lines together. Make sure the nylon wraps are tight. Complete the splice by coating with varnish or Pliobond.

9 Boater's Knots

Most fishermen at one time or another become "boaters," and some fishermen are boat-going fishermen all the time. Hence, while FISHERMEN'S KNOTS covers chiefly the knots needed with an angler's tackle, this chapter shows some of the knots frequently useful to the boat-going fisherman.

Many a fisherman has tied his skiff up to a dock, making a careless tie, and returned only to see the boat drifting away. Many another fisherman has tossed over an anchor, only to later retrieve just the rope—because of a careless tie.

The knots presented in this chapter are only a small presentation of "boaters'" knots, but they will well serve the fisherman who needs to know how to properly tie a line to a cleat, how best to fix an anchor, and so on.

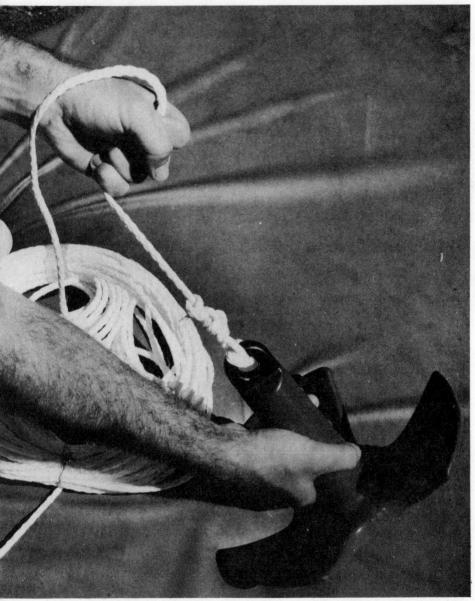

Losing an anchor can be inconvenient *and* expensive. The Anchor Hitch knot is a reliable line-to-anchor connection.

ANCHOR HITCH (Also called Fisherman's Bend and Anchor Bend)

Many experienced anglers consider this hitch the best for securing line to an anchor. The hitch can be tied and untied in a few seconds, and yet when properly fastened it will not slip or pull out.

To tie the Anchor Hitch, pass the line through the anchor ring twice, and then put the end of the line through the loop made by the line. Next tie two or three Half-Hitches onto the standing part of the line, and tighten.

EYE SPLICE

This is the best and strongest way of forming a loop in the end of rope. It seems complicated to make, but with practice it's easier to tie than it appears.

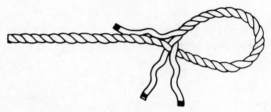

Fig. 1 Unwind about one foot of the strands that make up the end of the rope. Double the end of the rope back, and put one strand under any wrap of the standing part of the rope. Where you begin this determines the size of the loop formed.

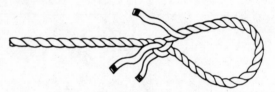

Fig. 2 Put another strand of rope under the wrap just above the first wrap.

Fig. 3 Turn the loop over . . .

Fig. 4 . . . and put the third strand of rope under the next wrap farther up the standing part of the rope. (A spike, nail, or even an ice pick is useful in lifting the wraps of the rope to insert the rope's strands under them.)

Fig. 5 Pull all three strands of rope taut.

Fig. 6 Continue alternately inserting the strands of rope under the wraps of the standing part of the rope. Do not tuck two strands of rope under the same wrap on the standing part of the line.

Fig. 7 The completed Eye Splice. At least three tucks should be made by each strand under different wraps of the standing part of the rope. Trim the strands when they become too short to make another tuck under the rope's wraps.

TWO HALF-HITCHES

This is a reliable and fast way of tying a rope to a piling for mooring a boat. It can be tied almost as quickly as a Half-Hitch, yet it is much stronger.

To make this connection wrap the rope twice around the piling, then wind the end of the rope twice around the standing part of the line, as shown.

SHEET BEND (Commonly called Single Sheet Bend)

The Sheet Bend is an adequate tie for joining two ropes of unequal diameter. It can be made quickly, and unties very readily. Too, it is strong enough to make it a practical knot that every boating angler should know.

Fig. 1 Double back the end of the larger rope. Insert the end of the small rope through the loop. Wrap the end of the small rope completely around both lines of the large rope. Then pass the end of the small rope back through the loop formed by the large rope.

Fig. 2 The completed Sheet Bend. After this knot is tied some anglers "lock" the Sheet Bend by tying a Half-Hitch with the end of the smaller rope onto the standing part of the smaller rope.

CLEAT COIL

Unused, coiled rope always is a problem to the boating angler. It gets in the way when walking around the boat or mooring, and it can be dangerous. The Cleat Coil is the easiest, neatest, and most efficient way to store rope until it's needed.

Fig. 1 Leave about three feet of rope leading from the cleat to the coils.

Fig. 2 Double the length of the rope leading from the coils to the cleat, and push it through the center of the coils, as shown.

Fig. 3 Twist the doubled rope two or three times.

Fig. 4 Bring the twisted line back over the coils and slip the last loop of the twisted rope over the cleat. The rope coils will be secured neatly to the cleat.

FIGURE EIGHT KNOT

Many anglers tie this knot in the end of all ropes leading from their boat. The Figure Eight Knot serves as a "stopper" which prevents other knots tied with the rope from "slipping."

It's easy to tie. Simply double the end of the rope, wrap the end around the standing part, and push the rope end out through the formed loop. Then pull on the end and standing part of the rope to tighten.

TIMBER HITCH

This is an amazingly strong hitch that can be tied very rapidly. It's used for securing a line from a boat to a piling.

The Timber Hitch is particularly popular among anglers who fish near bridges or in flooded timber areas. By employing the Timber Hitch they can link their boat's mooring ropes to a bridge support or tree limb, thus holding the boat in the best fishing position.

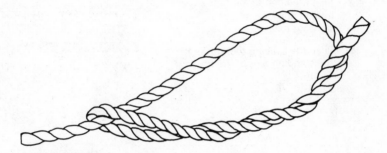

Fig. 1 Double the end of the rope back parallel to its standing part. Wind the end once around the standing part, then twist the rope end back on itself three times.

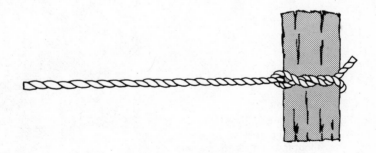

Fig. 2 Slip the noose over the piling and pull on the standing line to tighten.

DIAMOND-BRAIDED ROPE SPLICE

Diamond-braided rope is very popular among sport fishermen who own small boats. This type of rope is most often used by small boat fans because it is inexpensive yet is remarkably resistant to deterioration. However, tying knots with nylon or Dacron diamond-braided rope can be difficult. The Diamond-Braided Rope Splice is the easiest and best way to put a loop in the end of such ropes.

Fig. 1 Insert the end of the rope into an appropriate size splicing tool.

Fig. 2 Push the splicing tool through the standing part of the rope.

Fig. 3 Thread the splicing tool through the center of the standing part of the rope . . .

Fig. 4 . . . and then out of the standing part of the rope, about four inches from where the splicing tool was inserted.

Fig. 5 About two inches above where the splicing tool came out of the standing part of the rope, insert the tool once again into the center of the rope, as shown.

Fig. 6 Draw the end of the rope through the center of the standing part of the rope. Then withdraw the splicing tool so that the end of the rope remains within the standing part of the line.

Fig. 7 The completed Diamond-Braided Rope Splice is neat and very durable.

SHORT SPLICE

The Short Splice is the strongest, most reliable connection for joining two ropes of the same diameter. It takes time and patience to make this splice, but it is extremely secure.

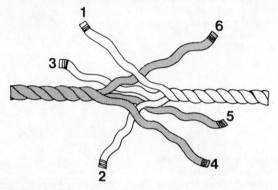

Fig. 1 Unravel all the lines making up a rope about six inches from the end of the rope. Whip the end of each line with waxed thread to keep them from unraveling. Then bring the two rope ends together, alternating the lines of one rope with the strands of the other rope.

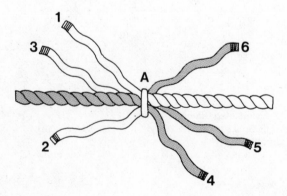

Fig. 2 Temporarily tie the two ropes together with another line at point A.

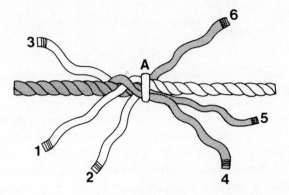

Fig. 3 Put strand 1 under the first wrap of the rope on the left, and pull strand 1 taut.

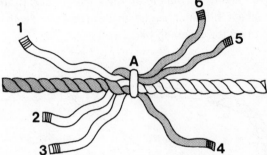

Fig. 4 Insert strand 2 under the next wrap of the left rope, and strand 3 under the third wrap. This completes one full "tuck" onto the left rope.

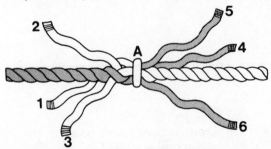

Fig. 5 Continue this process with the left rope until at least three full "tucks" are made. And do the same with other strands to the right-hand rope.

Fig. 6 Remove the temporary line at point A, trim the tag ends of all rope strands, and the Short Splice is finished.

SLIP KNOT

This is a sliding knot. It is no problem to tie in rope and it is very useful to boating fishermen. Often, anglers need a tie that will form a loop in the end of a length of rope, yet will "slide" to form a tight, secure connection. For example, many fishermen use the Slip Knot for linking their boat's bow and stern ropes to mooring posts. A large loop can be made, easily thrown over the post, then the loop can be tightened merely by pulling on the standing part of the rope.

To make a Slip Knot just tie an Overhand Knot with the end of the rope around the standing part of the rope.

BELAYING HITCH (Commonly called Belaying, Belaying To A Cleat, and Cleat Hitch)

Aimlessly winding rope around a cleat is not only the sign of a novice boating angler, it is often a very inefficient connection.

The Belaying Hitch is a superb tie for use with ropes that do not have a loop formed at the end. Too, this hitch is easy to do and is no problem to loosen.

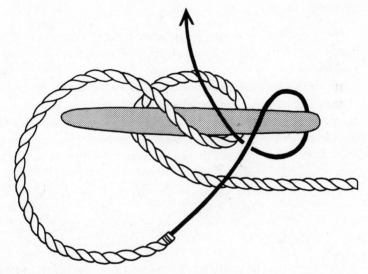

Fig. 1 Wind the rope once around the cleat. Bring the rope up diagonally over, and then under, the far end of the cleat.

Fig. 2 Pull the rope end diagonally back across the cleat again, wind it under the near end of the cleat, and tuck the rope end under the last cross over made by the rope.

WHIPPING A LINE

Whipping A Line keeps the end of a rope from fraying. This method is much quicker than Needle Whipping, but it is not as permanent.

The ends of most ropes should always be "whipped" before the rope is used. This must be done with manila rope, but rope made of synthetic fibers, such as nylon and Dacron, may be touched with a match, which will fuse their ends and keep them from unraveling.

Fig. 1 Form a loop in a waxed line. Lay the loop along the rope end. Wind the waxed line tightly around both the rope and the loop. The wraps are made away from the end of the rope.

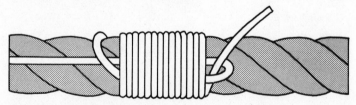

Fig. 2 Wrap the waxed line about 20 times around the rope and the loop, and insert the end of the waxed line through the loop.

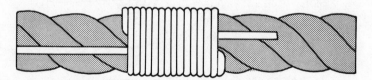

Fig. 3 Pull the end of the waxed line that forms the loop, so that both lines are drawn under the wraps. Then trim the two ends of the waxed line. The finished whipping can be lacquered or varnished if desired.

NEEDLE WHIPPING

This rope end whipping is time consuming. However, it is the best way to keep the end of a length of rope from fraying which, of course, prolongs the life of any rope.

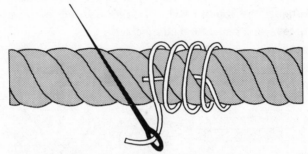

Fig. 1 Thread a sail-maker's needle with waxed line (waxing waterproofs the line.) Push the needle under one rope wrap and begin winding the waxed line back over itself.

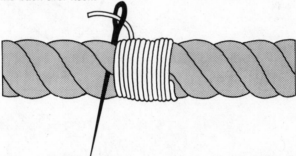

Fig. 2 Make 15 or 20 tight windings around the rope end with the waxed line. Thread the needle through the center of the rope at the end of the windings.

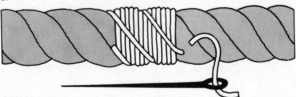

Fig. 3 Make two or three stitches through the rope with the waxed line, then trim the line close to the rope.

TUG BOAT HITCH (Also known as Tow-Boat Hitch)

The Tug Boat Hitch takes a little practice to learn to tie quickly. However, it is a very useful connection to boating anglers. If a boat must tow another boat with motor trouble, this is the hitch to use to connect the rope. It will not come undone, even under extreme stress, yet it can be untied quickly.

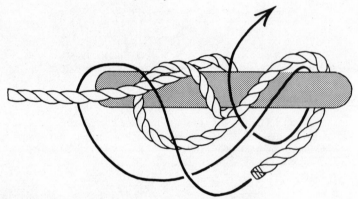

Fig. 1 Wind the end of the rope once around the towing post, then around the standing part of the rope and around the post again.

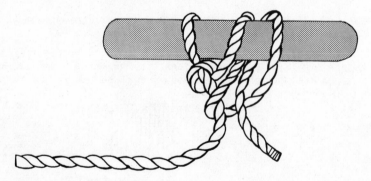

Fig. 2 Wrap the rope end around the standing part of the rope, around the post, and then tuck the rope end under the last cross over made by the rope end on the towing post.

Here are 14 Ranger bass boats—each secured to the dock with a Bowline Hitch.

BOWLINE KNOT (Also called Bowling Knot)

This is an outstanding knot to use in forming a loop in a length of line. The Bowline will not slip, and can be tied and untied easily.

It. is useful to anglers who need a loop in a rope for securing their fishing boat to a pier cleat or piling.

Fig. 1 Form a small loop in the standing part of the rope (how far the loop is formed from the end of the rope determines the size of the large loop.) Pass the end of the rope through the small loop.

Fig. 2 Turn the end of the rope around the standing part.

Fig. 3 Pass the end out through the loop.

Fig. 4 The completed Bowline Knot after drawing tight.

SQUARE KNOT (Sometimes referred to as Reef Knot)

This knot is a good one for securing two ropes temporarily. To make the knot, pass the left line over and under the right rope. Now put the line on the right over and under the other rope. Then tighten.

CLOVE HITCH

This is a quick, handy way of fastening a rope to a pier's piling. Thus, the Clove Hitch is used often by anglers who need a temporary way of securing boat ropes to a pier or dock.

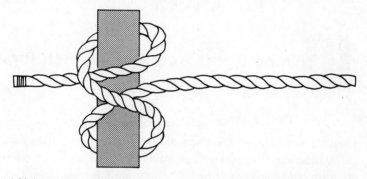

Fig. 1 Make a wrap with the rope end around the piling. Bring the end up and around the piling again, and tuck the rope end under the second wrap made by the rope.

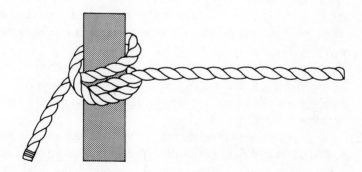

Fig. 2 Slide the two wraps together and the Clove Hitch is completed.

10 Good Knots and Playing Fish Right

All other factors equal, the knots are the weakest part of any fishing outfit. However, when the proper knot is used for a specific angling situation, and the knot is properly tied, the fisherman may fight a hooked fish to the limits of his tackle and be confident in the knowledge that "all will hold."

Many fishermen have little understanding of the extreme pressures their outfits can take. It doesn't matter if the fishing gear is fly, spinning, spincast, or bait casting; if it is rigged right, and good knots are tied, the tackle will take a lot of punishment before anything gives.

Wise fishermen are familiar with the amount of strain each of their fishing outfits will take. They know, for example, precisely how much pressure can be applied with a particular rod and line before one or the other breaks.

To familiarize yourself with the built-in "power" of your fishing outfits, tie their lines to a stationary object—something that can't be pulled loose—then, holding the rod at about the 3:00 o'clock position, tighten up and raise the rod. Keep putting a deep bend in the rod, and actually try to break the line. Do not snap the rod back and up, just apply a strong, steady, upwards pull. Unless you've got very light line, or have tied bad knots, you'll find that everything holds and that, in fact, you most likely cannot break the line no matter how hard you try. Such tests will show you precisely how tough your tackle really is, and that there is no need to "baby" fish you hook.

In learning to tie knots included in this book, it is worthwhile to test them as described above. Let's say, for example, that you've made up a fly fishing leader, using blood knots to connect the various strands, a nail knot to connect the leader butt to the fly line, and an improved clinch knot to tie the leader tippet to a fly. Set up your fly outfit, and hook the fly onto something solid. Now start to pull. If all the knots have been tied properly, you'll discover it is impossible to break the leader or to pull out a knot, unless of course, the leader tippet is super fine, testing a couple of pounds or less.

The same kind of "proofing" or testing of knots should be done with other tackle, too. Experienced tarpon fishermen, for example, do not make a cast, or put over their baits, until they've checked their tackle. Tarpon are a tremendous test of the fisherman's gear, and of how well he can tie knots. So most tarpon anglers, after having rigged up, attach their hooks to something solid, and then *pull, pull, pull*—and *pull* some more. When they're convinced everything will hold, they go fishing. Not before.

Fish that are hooked, no matter what the species, should not be "babied" but neither should they be "horsed." "Babying" is handling a fish so fearfully, so gently, that the fish barely exerts any pressure against the tackle; "horsing" is doing it the other way around, pulling on the fish so hard it doesn't have a chance to fight. The fisherman who consistently "horses" the fish he hooks is going to lose most of the good ones he gets on. Applying too much pressure too soon to a good fish is going to cause the hooks to pull out, line or rod to break, or for a knot to slip if it wasn't correctly tied.

Hooked fish should be fought according to the fish's size and its power, and according to the breaking point of the tackle. Skilled anglers fighting a fish strong enough to tax their tackle "play" the fish right up to a point just short of the breaking point of their gear; knowing how much strain their rod, reel, line, and knots will stand, they are able to fight the fish to the "tackle maximum."

His tackle is right, and all knots are tied perfectly, but this fly fisherman still must play his big pike properly before he'll put it in the boat.

Knowing how to play hooked fish is as important as rigging tackle correctly and tying knots fastidiously. It will do little good to become an expert fisherman and a knot-tying genius, only to lose the big fish you hook right at the boat because of some carelessness in playing the fish.

The first step in getting any fish into the boat is to set the hook properly. A lot of beginning fishermen, and some old-timers as well, do not understand that hooks must be "set" (driven) into fish, and that only rarely will a fish hook itself.

Use a rod that has enough backbone to sink hooks into fish when you pull back sharply on the rod as a fish strikes. In fishing for hard-mouth species—such as tarpon or muskies—use a rod with considerable backbone or stiffness; for soft-mouth fish—such as walleyes, trout, etc.—a rod with much lighter action can be used.

It takes a solid pull on the rod to sink hooks past the barb, and the larger the hook used, the more difficult it is to set it properly in a striking fish. The fishing line should be kept tight at all times, and the rod in a low position during retrieves. When a fish hits, the angler should raise his rod up and back, swiftly and with authority, in order to drive his hooks home.

In some kinds of fishing, many anglers "set" the hooks not once, but three, four, or more times. Hard-mouthed fish always should be "struck" by the angler several times. This includes muskies, tarpon, marlin, sailfish, etc.

When a fish is hooked right, half the battle is won; but after hooking, the fish still must be played out and then landed.

Never try to bring in a hooked fish by simply reeling. Instead, press the rod butt against your middle, and bring in line and the fish by the "pump-and-reel" method. To "pump" a fish, lower the rod tip and reel quickly to keep a tight line; then raise the rod smoothly, which will bring the fish toward you. Keep pumping and reeling to draw the fish close, but when he wants to go on a strong run, let him go.

Always let the rod and reel do the work in fighting a fish. By pumping and reeling, the rod will bend and flex, and thus tire the fish. The natural giving-taking action of the rod wears a fish down. And the drag on a reel also serves to beat a strong fish. When a hooked fish barrels off, taking line, he must pull it out against the reel's drag, and that can quickly exhaust him.

Try to keep fish from running out too much line. The more line between you and the fish you've hooked, the less pressure on the fish. When there's a lot of line out, you must first remove all the slack and stretch in the line before the hooked fish will feel any pull you exert. Always try to stay close enough to hooked fish to play them on short, tight lines.

A fish that is hooked right cannot get loose if he is in open water and is given slack line. However, a fish getting slack near roots or stumps can break off. Always keep a firm, tight line on fish fighting near snags. And whenever you hook a fish in weedy or snag-filled water, try to work him into the open as soon as possible.

Give slack line when the fish you've hooked jumps, especially if it's a big one. If you do not lower the rod tip, thus giving slack, when a large fish jumps, he may fall on the tight line and either break the line or pull the hooks out.

When hooked fish are brought close, they usually spook, making one more "last ditch" run. Be ready for it. If the fish makes a final, strong charge, just let him go. He'll only go a short way, and then will pause, and you can bring him right back again and land him readily.

When fish are properly played out they will lay on one side, right at the surface, fins fluttering weakly. They may be gently released then, or landed by netting, gaffing, or grasping by hand. Never put your fingers under the gill plate of a fish to be released, since this could injure it seriously.

Bass and trout can be landed easily by placing a thumb in the mouth, pressing down, then lifting. Such a grip paralyzes them, and they will not struggle. Muskies, pike, and walleyes have needle-like teeth, so are best landed by collaring from above, just behind the gill plates.

When preparing to boat a fish, do it sitting down. Leave a bit more than a rod's length of line out, then ease the fish to you by raising the rod up and back. If the fish doesn't come in readily he is not worn out enough. Let him go off again, and let the rod's action wear him down more.

When using a net to land a fish, place the net in the water and lead the fish into it head first. Never make quick, sweeping moves at a

A good-size Atlantic sailfish comes out of the ocean blue, stands on his tail, and glares at the angler. On such leaps, skilled anglers lower their rod tips so the fish will not fall on a tight line and break it.

hooked fish with a net; all this will do is spook him into a darting run, and he may break lose.

Regardless of how skillfully you hook and play fish, or how perfectly you tie knots, you are going to lose some. It's part of the game—the wonderful game of fishing!

Index